NINETY DAYS

Encouragement for the Christian Overeater

By

Pat N.

PRESS

This book is dedicated to my Lord and Savior Jesus Christ. I thank Him for loving me. I thank Him for rescuing my soul.

I also dedicate this book to my loving husband Jeff. Our six children (including spouses): Kurt, Amanda, Trisha, Jacob, Christina and Alex. And our two grandchildren: Kat and Matthew.

I give a special thanks to Christina who was my editor for this manuscript.

DAY 1

Forgetting what is behind and straining toward what is ahead, I press on toward the goal to win the prize for which God has called me heavenward in Christ Jesus.
Philippians 3:13,14

BEGIN AGAIN

I think back to that day in 1987 and wonder, "What if?" What if I had decided not to try just one more time? What if I had just given up and decided that it was too hard to get abstinent? Only God knew that making that one last effort to begin again, would result in (at this writing) over two decades of back-to-back abstinence.

Perhaps as you read this today you have had many false starts. Perhaps you are ashamed of letting your friends and family know that today is another day 1. Perhaps you hate yourself for breaking your abstinence and eating out of control again. Perhaps you are over weight and hate your body. Perhaps you are ashamed of how you obsess about food and eating all the time. Perhaps you have even wished that you were dead.

If any or all of these things apply to you then I would like you to know that God is all about new beginnings. If you know Jesus as Lord, you have the power inside to move mountains. He will give you the power to stop destroying yourself with the food. Regardless of what "the liar" tells you, the Lord <u>does</u> care about your abstinence. He wants you clean and powerful. He wants you following in His footsteps—helping the hopeless find hope.

He will show you how to be victorious. I urge you to get down on your knees. Call out to Him. Tell Him that you are ready to begin again—right now! Tell Him that you are not waiting for Monday, or after the wedding, or when the children are in school, or even tomorrow. Tell Him that you are ready to begin again this very moment.

{Father, thank you for all that You have given to me. Thank you for all that You have planned for my life. Help me not to be afraid. Give me faith to trust that You love me and You want me to succeed. Give me strength to follow Your call to my heart. I want abstinence today and everyday. I can not do this without You, and I cry out to You for the willingness and strength to press on and claim my victory. Jesus is Lord and I have my victory in Him! I pray in His name. Amen.}

Dig Deeper

- Are you a born again believer in the Lord Jesus Christ? If you are not, or you are not sure, go to <u>www. needhim.org</u>.
- When you search deep in your heart, do you know how it would look to eat in a God honoring way today? Write down your food plan for the next 24 hours.
- Read **2 Kings 19:14-16**. Take your food plan to the Lord and pray for victory over your "Assyria"—the stronghold of compulsive overeating.
- Pray that the Lord will bring a coach into your life that will encourage you and to whom you can be accountable.

DAY 2

**Anyone, then, who knows the good he ought to do
and doesn't do it, sins.
James 4:17**

SEEING MY SINFULNESS

When I was still overeating, I justified my misbehavior
by downplaying its severity. I told others and myself that
there were much worse things that I could be doing. I "joked"
that if I had to die (because everyone died) I might as well do
it enjoyably. "God made food," I said, "so let me have this
simple pleasure!"

If I was honest with myself, I could see that there was
nothing simple about how I related to the food. Overeating
was not an occasional pastime; it had become the major
activity in my day. Some aspect of eating was always on my
mind. I related to food with "passionate lust like the heathen,
who do not know God." (see 1 Thessalonians 4:3-8.)

In time, things became worse. My clothes did not fit. I
was winded by the smallest exertion. I began sneaking food
and telling lies so that others would not know how much I
could consume. I knew that I needed to get on a disciplined
regime of eating, but I told myself, "Tomorrow."

If I were to return to overeating, it would be sin. Eating
like that would waste time, waste money, and cause my body
to become distorted. Those who are lost would watch me and
wonder about the power of this God that I have said is Lord
of my life. My witness to them would be handicapped.

*{Dear Father, show me the areas in my life where I am trying
to justify sin. Give me eyes to see and a heart to obey. The
battle against these ungodly desires is wearing me down.*

Please quiet the fight within me. I pray to desire only You. I pray in the name of Jesus. Amen.}

Dig Deeper

- Read **James 4**. Underline verses and phrases that speak to your heart. Paraphrase one or more of these. Pray to apply today what God's word is saying to you.
- In what areas of your life is pride a frequent problem. Use a concordance to find several verses on humility. How does God's word speak to you?
- What things draw you closer to God? Have you done any of these things today?
- Eating in a way to keep your body lean and healthy requires prayers for willingness and strength. Have you asked the Lord to give you a plan for eating today that is God-honoring? Have you resolved to follow this plan whole-heartedly today?

DAY 3

Do not conform any longer to the pattern of this world, but be transformed by the renewing of your mind. Then you will be able to test and approve what God's will is—his good, pleasing and perfect will.
Romans 12:2

CHANGING MY THINKING

Much of my recovery is an inside job. Romans 12:2 reminds me not to be conformed any longer to the pattern of this world, but to be transformed by the renewing of my mind. This means that a greater part of my day needs to be spent filling my head with the things of God and putting into practice the things that He reveals through His Word.

It also means that I have to watch my interaction with the media. I cannot always read the newspaper. I sometimes have to get up and away from the television. I have to remember that most of what is so readily available for my eyes to see and my ears to hear has been authored and created by unbelievers. I have to be very cautious. My thinking can be influenced, and before I know it, my feelings are off.

I don't want to go back to a lifestyle that deadens me. I thank God for His written word and the many ways that I can fill my life with it.

{Dear Father, I pray to be obedient. Please give me the willingness and strength to live out your revealed word. Thank you, Lord, for bringing me out of slavery to sin. I pray to abide in Jesus so that I do not forget how abundantly you have blessed me. Please keep me sensitive to the temptation to backslide. Keep my head turned away from other gods. I pray in Jesus' name. Amen.}

Dig Deeper

- Read **Romans 12:1-8.** Underline verses and phrases that speak to your heart. Paraphrase one or more of these. Pray to apply today what God's word is saying to you.
- Can you honestly say that you love Jesus? Why or why not?
- In what areas of your life are you still worldly? Have you talked with the Lord about these?
- If God wrote out a "to do" list for you today, what might be some of the items on the list?
- What things do you do well? When did you last use them for the glory of God?
- How has the disease been calling you back lately?

DAY 4

*They are blind guides. If a blind man leads a blind man,
both will fall into a pit. Matthew 15:14*

BLIND GUIDES

Even before I could help myself, I had this deep desire to be of help to others. I was especially sensitive to those who were struggling with weight and/or overeating issues. I subconsciously believed that if I could motivate others to do what was right, then I could motivate myself. I did not see this as putting the cart before the horse.

Jesus says: *"Why do you look at the speck of sawdust in your brother's eye and pay no attention to the plank in your own eye? How can you say to your brother, 'Let me take the speck out of your eye,' when all the time there is a plank in your own eye? You hypocrite, first take the plank out of your own eye, and then you will see clearly to remove the speck from your brother's eye."* (Matthew 7:3-5)

I had a plank in my own eye, and it was called pride. I liked telling others how to get their life in order because it could let me forget about the chaos and disorder in my own life. However, without the wisdom of God, I was adding to the misery of others. I was a blind guide.

As a maturing Christian, I am beginning to see that it's never about me helping in my own power. It is about being a servant of the Lord Jesus Christ. He alone has the wisdom of knowing what is needed. He alone provides the power to walk alongside another and not merely point the way.

{Thank you for the indwelling Spirit who teaches me and empowers me. Thank you, Father, for the many times you have allowed me to lovingly guide another. I pray to give

*You the glory and praise whenever another is helped by my
obedience. In Jesus' name I pray. Amen.}*

Dig Deeper

- *Read **Matthew 23:23-28.*** Underline verses and
  phrases that speak to your heart. Paraphrase one or
  more of these. Pray to apply today what God's word
  is saying to you.
- Write about the people who sadden you as you see
  them struggling with food and weight issues. How is
  your present recovery helping them?
- Who are the people that you always seem to be giving
  advice? Do you share with them in the first person or
  do you "point out the gap" without offering to be a
  yokefellow? Do you need to make amends for your
  behavior in this regard?
- Are you concerned about a child or younger sibling
  who seems to be following in your overeating
  "footsteps?" Write out a prayer to God about your
  concerns.

DAY 5

So if you have not been trustworthy
in handling worldly wealth,
who will trust you with true riches?
Luke 16:11

WASTING MONEY

Wasting money and overeating compulsively went hand-in-hand with me. Financing a binge took money. If I ate the food on hand, I had to replace it before others in the household went looking for it. If I went out, looking to satisfy a craving, I could REALLY do damage. The "magic muffin" was often so elusive. I have many memories of walking the aisles of supermarkets eating from opened bags and searching for the perfect binge ingredients. I often ended up not only wasting money but also throwing away valuable time by the handful.

Money that should have been spent to pay bills left my account at record speed. It was sometimes as if I had amnesia. I could not always remember when and what I spent. I had plans of being a better money manager, just like I had plans to eat better. Unfortunately, all plans for improved behavior flew out of the window once the craving began.

Because Jesus is now Lord of my life, I own nothing. In Galatians 2:20, Paul says it this way: *"I have been crucified with Christ and I no longer live, but Christ lives in me. The life I live in the body, I live by faith in the Son of God, who loved me and gave himself for me."*

It's no longer my money. It's God's money. It's not about indulging my pleasures. It's about serving God by ministering to His people.

{Dear Father, I pray that I am finished with wasting money. I pray to turn to you when I have a craving. Please teach me to find my delight in you alone. Fill me with your love and empower me to give unselfishly to those in need. I pray in Jesus' name. Amen.}

Dig Deeper

- Read **Luke 16:10-13.** Underline verses and phrases that speak to your heart. Paraphrase one or more of these. Pray to apply today what God's word is saying to you.
- Besides wasting money on the food itself, what other ways has your overeating affected your finances? Are you truly done with squandering God's money?
- Using a concordance, look up verses in the Bible that deal with money. Summarize some of what you learned.
- Who are some good managers of money that you know? What skills and mindset do they possess that might be a good thing to acquire in your own life?

DAY 6

Look to the LORD and his strength; seek his face always.
Remember the wonders he has done, his miracles,
and the judgments he pronounced.
1 Chronicles 16:11, 12

REMEMBERING WHAT GOD HAS DONE

Sometimes life seems very, very heavy. I can't seem to shake the feeling that there is too much to do and no time to do it. Before long I start to feel sorry for myself, and I start acting as if God has forgotten me. I worry and my prayers become short and more from my head and less from my heart. I lose my focus and wander very close to the "edge of night." This is a very dangerous place to be.

But God is so good. Through His word, the Bible, He urges me to remember. He shows me many times when His people had wandered away from Him and He lovingly guided them back to Himself. He brings to my mind the many times when He has done the same thing in my life. He assures me of His never-ending love and care for me.

Remembering what God has done blesses me. I am filled to overflowing with gratitude, hope, and joy.

{Dear Father, I pray to continually seek Your face. Reveal to me the legacy of Your love in my life. Teach me how to abide in Jesus more and more each day. It's in His name that I pray. Amen.}

Dig Deeper

- Read **1 Chronicles 16:8-12.** Underline verses and phrases that speak to your heart. Paraphrase one or more of these. Pray to apply today what God's word is saying to you.
- How is your walk with the Lord today?
- Tell of some marvelous things that Lord has done in your past. How are you being blessed by Him today?
- Are you eating in a God-honoring way today? How might you talk to the Lord about the way you are eating today?
- What are some of the ways that you practice abiding in the Lord?

DAY 7

Let us fix our eyes on Jesus,
the author and perfecter of our faith,
who for the joy set before him endured the cross,
scorning its shame,
and sat down at the right hand of the throne of God.
Hebrews 12:2

NOT LOSING GROUND

God has laid out a path of life for me to follow. Every step of progress that I make along The Way is important to Him. He has not sent me out alone. The Bible has recorded many examples of faithful and holy people from whom I draw lessons of living. In addition, I have modern-day Christians who have lived and are living their lives victoriously. I am encouraged to join them in letting my light shine for the glory of God.

There are defects of character that have the potential of slowing me down and hindering my progress. With the Lord's help, I must work at letting these go. I must keep my resolve to do all I can to not lose ground.

Keeping my commitment to eat in a God-honoring way is essential in this determination to continue forward. My abstinence is important to Jesus. To overeat compulsively would be to turn my back on the lessons of faith that I am being taught. Excess food has no potential to solve life's problems; only Jesus can do this. Excess food only slows down my progress and causes me to try in vain to serve two masters.

{Dear Father, I pray not to let anything distract me from Jesus and His purpose for my life. I pray to keep Him before me throughout this day. It's in His name that I pray. Amen.}

Dig Deeper

- Read **Hebrews 12:1-4.** Underline verses and phrases that speak to your heart. Paraphrase one or more of these. Pray to apply today what God's word is saying to you.
- How do you define "compulsive overeating?" Do you still overeat compulsively at times? Do you see it as sinful behavior? Why or why not?
- List some behaviors that continue to slow you down toward the goal of being "sold out to Jesus." Is this a goal for you? If not, why not?
- Read **Hebrews 11** to learn more about the "cloud of witnesses" mentioned in Hebrews 12:1. Who are your encouragers? Who are the ones that you encourage?

DAY 8

Therefore each of you must put off falsehood
and speak truthfully to his neighbor,
for we are all members of one body.
Ephesians 4:25

RIGOROUS HONESTY

In the flesh, I tell a lie and try to cover it up. I tell myself that I am protecting the feelings of another. Or, I try not to think about it. Or, I tell myself that whatever I'm being deceitful about is not THAT important. Thankfully, I cannot hide behind these rationalizations very long. God is giving me a very thin skin when it comes to dishonesty. I become restless, and I feel out of step with the Lord.

Jesus called the devil, "the father of lies" (John 8:44). If I am serious in my desire to grow in godliness, I must be through with lying. I cannot practice it. I cannot excuse it. I must throw myself on the mercy of God to stop.

When I am tempted to tell a lie (or after I have lied), it helps me to pray in this manner: "God give me the willingness and the strength to do the right and truthful thing." I am God's child, and I can trust Him to give me the desire to be obedient and the ability to carry out His plan (see Philippians 2:13).

Jesus knows perfectly how to speak the truth in love, and I want to be like Jesus. As I abide in Him, He empowers me to be honest in all my affairs.

{Dear Father, many times I tell a lie in an attempt to avoid the anger or the disapproval of others. It's unfruitful to live this way. Thank you for convicting my heart of my sin. Make me a master at speaking the truth in love. I pray these things in the name of Jesus. Amen.}

Dig Deeper

- *Read **Ephesians 4:24-26.*** Underline verses and phrases that speak to your heart. Paraphrase one or more of these. Pray to apply today what God's word is saying to you.
- Have you made a commitment to follow a God-honoring way of eating today? If you deviate off this plan, would you see it as dishonest? Why or why not?
- What is God teaching you about honesty? What are some verses that help you?
- Tell of a time when the Spirit empowered you to speak the truth in love? If it wasn't received well, what was your response?

DAY 9

*Peace I leave with you; my peace I give you. I do not give
to you as the world gives. Do not let your hearts
be troubled and do not be afraid.*
John 14:27

TRUE PEACE

I was a binge eater. Sometimes, I had no idea why I binged. Other times, I knew exactly why—something bothered me greatly, and I used the food as a means of escape. In other words, I allowed my heart to become troubled and full of fear. When fear filled my heart, the peace of God eluded me.

The world around me believes that peace is an outer endeavor. Popular teaching is that peace will come about as one figures out a solution and works out the details. God is totally left out of the equation. I have tried this peace-attaining method, and I can attest to the truth that it doesn't work! As someone has said, "No Jesus, no peace. Know Jesus, know peace."

God wants to be deeply involved in every aspect of my life. As a Christian, if I'm disturbed in my spirit, I don't need more food; I need more intimate interactions with my Savior. In the long run, overeating never solves anything in my life. Overeating complicates my life and worsens my predicament.

{Dear Lord, I pray to cry out from my heart to You at the first sign of unrest. I pray to listen, expectedly, to hear You speak to me through Your word. Thank you for the gift of salvation. Because of You I know the peace that passes understanding. You have given my heart a hiding place, Jesus, and I am so, so grateful.}

Dig Deeper

- Read **John 14:23-27.** Underline verses and phrases that speak to your heart. Paraphrase one or more of these. Pray to apply today what God's word is saying to you.
- When was the last time you had a binge? What were the circumstances that led up to this happening? Have you spoken to God about your binge eating—past and/or present?
- What things trouble you most often? What is your favorite verse that reminds you to stay in the peace of God and away from worry? Use a site such as Bible Gateway to find 3 or more versions of your favorite verse. Print them out and place them where you can see them today.
- Think back to when you first gave your heart and your life to Jesus. Are you even closer to Him today than you were then? Why or why not?

DAY 10

For God did not give us a spirit of timidity,
but a spirit of power,
of love and of self-discipline.
2 Timothy 1:7

EMBRACING DISCIPLINE

When I was deep into compulsive overeating, I wanted no restrictions on my food intake. My dream was to find a way to eat all that I wanted and still be "skinny." I thought that a food plan would take away the pleasures of eating. I thought if I put controls on my food, I would have to be shut off from the world, never enjoying meals with my family and friends. How wrong I was! As I have learned to stay true to my commitment to abstinence, I have found the joy of guilt-free eating.

These are some disciplines that God gives me daily to help keep my food in order:

1. I eat only three measured meals a day to clear my body of compulsive overeating and my mind of obsessive thinking about the food. I do this because overeating had become a form of idolatry in my life.

2. I don't eat some foods at all because they have a history of becoming "larger than life" to me.

3. I check in daily with an accountability partner because it helps me to stay honest with the food.

4. I pray to have a quality quiet time each day. I meet with God at the beginning of the day in order to give Him the "first fruits" of each 24 hours.

5. With God's help, I pray with sincerity and thanksgiving before each meal. I need the conscious reminder throughout the day that it is only by His grace that I am not compulsively overeating today.

6. I try to keep the "Great Commission" (Matthew 28:16-20) before me daily. I am called to bring the good news to the lost and encouragement to the saved.

7. I prayerfully resolve to make each day the very best it can be—for Jesus' sake. I no longer assume that I have the guarantee of tomorrow.

{Thank you, Father, for the power to stay abstinent today. Thank you for skills to be disciplined and God-honoring in my eating. You are such a wonderful God, and I praise You for loving me so much. It's in the name of Jesus that I pray. Amen.}

Digging Deeper

- Read **2 Timothy 1:6,7.** Underline words and phrases that speak to your heart. Look up the definitions of key words. Write a paraphrase of this passage and make a plan to put God's message into action.

- Write out some of the disciplines that help you to stay clean and clear with your food. Have you asked the Lord for strength to have integrity in your eating today?

- What foods do you find hard to eat in a God-honoring way? Are these foods still on your food plan? Why or why not?

DAY 11

Do not merely listen to the word, and so deceive
yourselves. Do what it says.
James 1:22

INTO ACTION

In earlier times, one of my favorite things to do was to read about diets. It was as if I believed that the pounds would just fall off as I filled myself with the knowledge of how to lose weight. Needless to say, I remained overweight and struggling. I had to move past just knowing what to do about my compulsive overeating to actually putting what I was learning into action.

Growing in my faith has the same requirement. God has given me His word so that I might have life; however, if I merely know what the Bible says and fail to practice what it teaches, then I am just fooling myself. The blessings come in doing what God asks regardless of how inconvenient it is or how scary it seems.

God's word points out His path of life. God's Spirit fills me with the willingness and strength to do what His word says.

{Dear Father, I pray to put your word into action today. Convict me when I am stockpiling your revelations and not applying them. Please, Father, give me the willingness and the strength to grow in obedience. I pray this in Jesus' name. Amen.}

Digging Deeper

- Read **James 1:22-25.** Underline words and phrases that speak to your heart. Look up the definitions of key words. Write a paraphrase of this passage and make a plan to put God's message into action.
- Are you growing in your faith? Are you growing in obedience? How do you measure your progress in both these areas?
- What methods do you use to help you apply consistently what you learn in the word of God?

DAY 12

Be self-controlled and alert. Your enemy the devil prowls around like a roaring lion looking for someone to devour.
1 Peter 5:8

PERSEVERANCE

When things got tough, really tough, I would always manage to find my way back into the food. The thought before the binge was that I needed something to relax me and make me "happy". For a while I believed the lie—that overeating was going to do both of these things. But before long, I could not hide from the truth that overeating neither relaxed me nor made me happy. Instead, overeating eventually brought on physical discomfort, mental self-condemnation, tiredness, and distortion of my body.

When things get out of control, the Bible reminds me to be self-controlled. The evil one is not sleeping; he is waiting for his opportunity to come in for the kill. The Bible reminds me to stand firm in the faith, knowing that the power in me is greater than the power leveled against me.

I am called to persevere in my suffering. My present discomfort is nothing compared to what Jesus endured to make me God's child. On the other side of my trial, I will be restored and strengthened.

{Dear Father, I pray to trust you through my trials. I pray not to run after false gods looking for the comfort that only You can give. I pray to talk to You honestly about my anxiety and fears and wait for the return of Your peace. Draw me closer to You each day. Comfort me, as only You can. I pray in Jesus' name. Amen.

Digging Deeper

- Read **1 Peter 5:7-9**. Underline words and phrases that speak to your heart. Look up the definitions of key words. Write a paraphrase of this passage and make a plan to put God's message into action.
- Are you presently going through a period of suffering? Are you allowing the Lord to teach you humility through these circumstances? Are you spending these trying times in the word of God or are you whining and complaining?
- How are your food choices in stressful times? Are you depending on the high calorie "goodies" to get you through, or is the Lord your shelter in the storm?
- Have you given much thought today to those who are being persecuted world-wide for the cause of Christ? Are you willing to pray for them today? Right now?

DAY 13

No temptation has seized you except what
is common to man. And God is faithful; he will not
let you be tempted beyond what you can bear.
But when you are tempted, he will also provide
a way out so that you can stand up under it.
1 Corinthians 10:13

STANDING THROUGH TEMPTATION

The devil uses temptation to divert me from righteous behavior. Temptation is sometimes subtle and covert. It is sometimes brazen and "in my face."

There is a part of me that is embarrassed by temptation. This part erroneously believes that with enough spiritual growth I won't have to deal with being tempted ever again. The truth is that as long as I live in this body, I will always have to deal with temptation.

The glorious truth is that I never have to deal with temptation alone and in my own strength. God has placed His Spirit in my heart, which is stronger than any attack from the enemy.

{Dear Father, thank you for loving me so much. Thank you for the strength you have given me to stand against temptation. I pray never to put your power to the test. I pray never to foolishly court temptation by deliberately placing myself in sin's path. Keep me prayerfully close to you at all times. In Jesus' name I pray. Amen.}

Digging Deeper

- Read **1 Corinthians 10:12-14**. Underline words and phrases that speak to your heart. Look up the definitions of key words. Write a paraphrase of this passage and make a plan to put God's message into this day.
- Lately, have you been giving in to the temptation to overeat? Does "your brand" of temptation seem unusually hard or unique? How do you interpret 1 Corinthian 10:13 in regards to your personal food struggles? What are some of the ways out of the temptation to overeat have you not been willing to try before? Are you willing to pray for willingness?
- Who are the people that help you to resist temptation? How might you enlist their help more? In what ways might you help someone close by who is being tempted?

DAY 14

Simon Peter answered him, "Lord, to whom shall we go?
You have the words of eternal life."
John 6:68

NO TURNING BACK

My life was once characterized as always having this deep, deep yearning for purpose and place. I did not know it, but I was seeking to have an intimate relationship with God. God and His will for my life was one big mystery. There were times when I felt His love, but these times were often fleeting. I had no idea how to please God all of the time.

Today, I know that Jesus became the supreme sacrifice so that I could be reconciled to God eternally. He is the Son of God. When I, a sinner, received Jesus as my Savior and Lord, my peace was made with God. When God looks at me, He sees His redeemed child, and I am pleasing to Him. It's all because of Jesus.

Jesus is everything to me. I can do nothing of eternal value accept through Him. He is my joy. He is my peace.

{Thank you, Father, for sending your Perfect Lamb to save me. Thank you for giving me the faith to accept your gift of love. I give you my praise, with all of my heart, in Jesus' name. Amen.}

Digging Deeper

- Read **John 6:67-69**. Underline words and phrases that speak to your heart. Look up the definitions of key words. Write a paraphrase of this passage and make a plan to put God's message into this day.
- Have you been having success with food and/or weight control, yet still feeling a deep apartness? What does Jesus mean to you?
- What are some of the ways you have tried in the past to reach a deeper relationship with God? Did you ever have a close relationship with Jesus? Do you know anyone who does? How would you describe their life and manner of living?
- How do you define eternal life? Do you have it?

DAY 15

Praise be to the God and Father of our Lord Jesus Christ,
the Father of compassion and the God of all comfort, who
comforts us in all our troubles, so that we can comfort
those in any trouble with the comfort
we ourselves have received from God
2 Corinthians 1:3,4

THE RIGHT RESPONSE

Bad things are going to happen to me even when I have not brought them on by my misbehavior. When these bad things happen I can respond in one of three ways: a) get mad at God, while pouting and feeling sorry for myself, b) try, to the point of distraction, to figure out why this bad stuff is happening to me, or c) pray.

Two of the ways prolong my misery. One brings relief.

For me, the right response to suffering is prayer. This leads me to think of how my situation might be of help to another who is going through the same struggle. I am blessed as I reach out toward them with compassion.

{Dear Father, I pray to remember that faith means total reliance upon you– even when I don't totally understand my situation. I thank you for my salvation. Through it, I experience your eternal love for me. Thank you, Jesus, for being with me in the midst of my difficulties. I give you thanks and praise. Amen.}

Digging Deeper

- Read **2 Corinthians 1:3-5.** Underline words and phrases that speak to your heart. Look up the definitions of key words. Write a paraphrase of this passage and make a plan to put God's message into this day.
- What are your present troubles? How have you prayed to the Lord regarding these? Are you trying to use food to comfort you? Have you ever used food in the past? How well did it work?
- Describe a time when you felt an abundance of God's comfort to you. Has there ever been a time when you were able to comfort another unselfishly?

DAY 16

O Sovereign LORD, remember me.
O God, please strengthen me just once more.
Judges 16:28

LEARNING THE HARD WAY

The story of Sampson in Judges 13-16 reminds me that sometimes I have to learn things the hard way. Sampson had many blessings, but he squandered them with riotous living. God had to bring him to the end of himself before he saw the light. The same was true with me and overeating.

In the beginning, I saw overeating as a way to have fun—a way to relax and have a good time. In the end, I was always "off my diet". My body became sick and bloated by the quantity of sugar and starches that I poured into it. I became a loner. I kept people at "arms length" because I didn't want them to discover the abnormal things I did with food. I started to do a lot of lying and hiding—from others and from myself.

I was depressed most of the time. I tried to diet, but before the day was over, I was bingeing again. I had deep wishes to be anywhere other than in my own skin. I began to scare myself with the thoughts that came into my head.

This type of living brought me to the end of myself. I see today that in His love, God allowed the food to give me quite a beating. Sometimes it "takes what it takes."

{Thank you, Father, for the last beating that you allowed me to experience with the food. Today I remember my last binge, and I don't ever want to live that way again. Thank you for my abstinence. In Jesus' name, I pray. Amen.}

Digging Deeper

- Read the story of Samson in **Judges 13-16.** Retell the story in your own words. What lessons do you learn?
- The dictionary defines an addiction as "an uncontrollable compulsion to repeat a behavior regardless of its negative consequences." Do you have an overeating addiction?
- How is Samson's sexual addiction like your addiction to overeating?
- When was the last time you cried out for God's mercy as Samson did in Judges 16:28? What were your circumstances? What was the outcome? Are you in need of God's mercy today? Are you willing to pray for the willingness?

DAY 17

Despite their fear of the people around them,
they built the altar on its foundation and sacrificed
burnt offerings on it to the LORD.
Ezra 3:3

RISING ABOVE FEELINGS OF FEAR

I used to have a terrible time staying true to a food plan. Many times fear was the reason I lost my resolve to stay away from certain foods. I was fearful of what others might say. Even more, I was fearful of what others might be thinking about me.

But God is very, very good. He provided models of courage. I found myself in the company of people who had acquired the skill of planning what they ate and eating what they planned. They did this without exception, no matter what the circumstance. It didn't matter. Even if they didn't FEEL like practicing integrity with the food, they did it anyway. Their example showed me how it could be done. In time, I, too, acquired the skill of not letting my feelings control my abstinence.

Jesus wants my behavior to be God-honoring. This includes my behavior with the food. I trust the Lord to give me both the willingness and the strength to stay abstinent today. For this, I am very grateful and give God the praise!

{Dear Lord, no one or no thing is more important than You. Thank you for teaching me that I can eat in a God-honoring way regardless of circumstances. Strengthen me to resist feelings of fear and to stand firm. It's in your name that I pray. Amen.}

Digging Deeper

- Read **Ezra 3.** Retell the story in your own words. What lessons do you learn?
- Use a dictionary and write a definition of "integrity." Think over your eating behavior in the past week. Have you practiced integrity with the food? If not, would you write and pray a prayer for willingness to eat in a God-honoring way for the next 24 hours?
- In this chapter, despite the hard times, the people gave praise to God. When did you last give praise to God through a hard time? What happened as a result of your obedience?

DAY 18

My dear brothers; take note of this: Everyone should be quick to listen, slow to speak and slow to become angry.
James 1:19

QUICK TO LISTEN

God speaks to me through His word. Yet, there have been times when I have delayed taking action on what His word has revealed to my heart. It's sad to think that one day Jesus might need to show me many missed opportunities I lost to procrastination.

I would be a hopeless case without prayers in Jesus' name. I am learning to ask for willingness and strength to do that which seems hard or unpleasant. God is so faithful. I have seen Him move me through an inability to budge or even think because I feel so overwhelmed. Step by step, He has led me through many tasks that seemed impossible.

What an awesome God I serve. He never leaves me powerless to do that which He calls me to obey.

{Dear Father, thank you for working in me to obey you. I pray to mature daily so that I might respond quickly to your promptings to my heart. It's in the name of Jesus that I pray. Amen.}

Digging Deeper

- Read **James 1:19-21.** Underline words and phrases that speak to your heart. Look up the definitions of key words. Write a paraphrase of this passage and make a plan to put God's message into this day.
- Think about your eating in the past few days. Are there actions that you need to be taking in order to

have a cleaner and more committed abstinence? Have you asked God to show you attitudes that need revision? Have you prayed for willingness and strength to obey?

* Are you reading and studying the word of God daily? If not, are their activities that you are doing daily that could possibly be shortened to allow for these vital Christian disciplines?

DAY 19

A new command I give you: Love one another.
As I have loved you,
so you must love one another.
John 13:34

THE FEVER OF SELF LOVE

The world gives many instructions regarding self love. I am told to protect my "boundaries" and to "look out for number one" because "I'm worth it!" I can remember one diet technique where I was told to stand in front of the mirror without clothes. Cradling each part of my body, I was to say, "I love you." This exercise was to eventually stop my over-eating by teaching me how to love myself. These methods failed miserably.

The Bible says that I love because Jesus first loved me. (1 John 4:19) I never knew true love until I was saved by grace. Jesus became the perfect sacrifice for my transgressions; therefore, I want to please Him out of a deep gratitude that I feel for my salvation. Nothing pleases Jesus more that to love others as He has loved me.

Listening to the world, I can work myself crazy trying to find self-satisfaction. Yet, nothing that the world offers can even come near to the joy I have in knowing Jesus. In Him alone is the "fever" broken, and I am made whole.

{Thank you for opening my eyes to the insanity of self-satisfaction. Thank you, Father, for giving me your Son. Because of Him I have a firm place to stand. Because of Him I have a glorious new song to sing. Thank you, Father. Thank you, Jesus.}

Digging Deeper

- Read **1 John 4:7-21.** List the things that you learn about love from this passage.
- Do you know the true satisfaction of serving others in the power and love of Jesus? Describe how different this is from serving others before you were saved.
- What were some of the vain attempts you had at trying to control your overeating without the Lord? How is God-honoring eating helping you to walk selflessly?

DAY 20

Those who cling to worthless idols forfeit the grace
that could be theirs.
Jonah 2:8

FOOLISHNESS AND PAIN

Jonah was a prophet of God. God had given him a mission to go to Nineveh and preach to the people there in hopes that they would repent from their evil ways. Jonah hated the people of Nineveh. He wanted to see them punished.

He didn't like God's plan and decided to carry out one of his own. He tried to run from God, but God found him on a ship heading in the totally opposite direction from Nineveh. God sent a storm that frightened the other men on the ship so much that they feared for their life.

The men cast lots to see who might be responsible for the tragedy, and the lot fell on Jonah. When the men came to him, Jonah openly admitted that he was a Hebrew and that He was running away from God. Jonah was so in love with "his way" that he was willing to die rather than to obey the will of God. He told the men to throw him overboard.

Long before I surrendered to this God-given plan of eating that I now follow, I fought it. I thought that there must surely be something more to my liking. Over and over again, I tried to be abstinent on my own and following my own way. "My own way" was a worthless idol. It took many years of foolishness and pain before I embraced "weighing and measuring without exception" and saw it as a blessing and not a curse. I pray never to deprive myself of this wonderful gift of freedom.

{Thank you, Father, for the many times that you have rescued me from my foolishness. I pray to be forever through with compulsive overeating. Thank you for my abstinence. I trust you for the willingness and strength to take the necessary actions to stay clean, clear, and committed today. It is in the name of Jesus that I pray. Amen.}

Digging Deeper.

- Read **Jonah 1-3**. Write down all that you can remember from the story. Do you identify with Jonah? Why or why not? What things do you learn about God in this book?
- Is there is something about which you are being stubborn? Have you prayed about it? Have you shared honestly with a prayer partner about it? Have you prayed together about the situation?
- Have you ever been angry with God? Are you angry with him today? Have you ever tried to run away from God? Share about the lessons you learned from your foolishness.

DAY 21

*"I tell you," he replied, "if they keep quiet,
the stones will cry out."
Luke 19:40*

PRAISE RUNNING OVER

One day, Peter and John encountered a lame man on their way into the temple. The man was a beggar who was brought there with hopes of getting money from those passing through.

When Peter saw him, he said with authority, "Rise in the name of Jesus." He took the man by the hand and lifted him to his feet. The man was immediately healed. Out of joy and gratitude, the once-lame man began to leap and hop around. Before long, the crowd heard of this miracle and they gathered at the temple. Peter used this opportunity to preach about the Good News of our Lord and brought many, many more to Christ.

Peter and John were arrested for disturbing the peace, but the officials were afraid to do much more for fear of angering the crowd. The next day, they were released with the warning not to speak in Jesus' name. But they replied, "We cannot help speaking about what we have seen and heard" (Acts 4:20).

Whenever I experience something wonderful, I can't keep my mouth closed about it. This is certainly true about being set free from the food. The same thing is happening in regards to my new birth in Jesus.

Salvation is not for the few — God wants the masses to be saved. Like Peter, I cannot help speaking about this miracle. It is bubbling over in me, and I pray that my witness brings others to the Lord.

{Dear Father, I pray to let my life shout of the salvation you have given to me. Please fill me with the Holy Spirit. I pray for courage to witness and share the Good News. It is in the name of Jesus that I pray. Amen}

Digging Deeper

- Read **Luke 19:37-40.** Underline words and phrases that speak to your heart. Look up and write down the definitions of key words. Write a paraphrase of this passage and make a plan to put God's message into this day.
- Read **Acts 3-4:22.** Re-tell the story in your own words. Write about the lessons you learn in this passage. Pray and ask God to show you where you need to make application in your own life.
- Who helped you to become abstinent? Some people believe that the best way to bring abstinence to another is through our own clean commitment to abstinence. Do you agree? Why or why not?

DAY 22

*Though the fig tree does not bud and there are no grapes
on the vines, though the olive crop fails and the field
produce no food, though there are no sheep in the pen
and no cattle in the stalls, yet I will rejoice in the LORD,
I will be joyful in God my savior. Habakkuk 3:17, 18*

TRUSTING JESUS THROUGH HARD TIMES

When thing got bad, I ate. It took the example of others
to show me that I did not have to break my abstinence just
because life was not happening the way I thought it should.
They shared how they were learning that, even though
circumstances in life often moved beyond their control,
they didn't have to eat about it. They modeled how to stay
committed to weighing and measuring, without exception,
no matter what.

I am learning to have the same resolve about trusting God
in hard times. Many times, life throws hard punches. The
battering seems endless. But Jesus is with me through it all.

Jesus loves me no matter what. When life stinks and I'm
hurting all over, when people hate me and the money is gone,
when the enemy seems to be winning and I am exhausted,
Jesus loves me.

When life seems the worse it can be, I remember that I
belong to Jesus. He warned that life would have tribulations.
But He has assured me that there is a day coming when my
grief will turn into joy. (see John 16:20-33)

*{Dear Lord, I pray to always know that you love me.
Strengthen me in the hard times. Teach me how to fix my
eyes on You. Let me say with unwavering confidence that
nothing can separate me from Your love. I pray this in Your
holy name. Amen.}*

Digging Deeper

- Read **Habakkuk 1:1-3:19**. Use a modern translation or a commentary to get an understanding of what is happening in this book. Choose a verse to memorize this week.
- Are you still eating over the ups and downs of life? What, if anything, are you learning from you experience?
- Are there things happening in your life that seem unfair? Are you reacting in fear or responding in truth? Have you deprived yourself of the comfort and help that the Lord is providing to get you through?

DAY 23

*"What they are building—if even a fox climbed up on it,
he would break down their wall of stones!"*
Nehemiah 4:3

DEALING WITH DISCOURAGEMENT

In the fourth chapter of Nehemiah, the Israelites, under Nehemiah's leadership, have begun to rebuild Jerusalem's wall. As the project gets on its way, two onlookers, Sanballet and Tobiah, begin to mock their efforts and try to hinder their progress.

Instead of giving up, the builders turn to the LORD in prayer and continue to work with all their heart. Eventually, they not only finish the wall, but they complete the project in record time.

Recently, I heard a Bible teacher say that discouragement, in his opinion, was the devil's favorite weapon. There have been times in my life when I have been criticized and have given up. I can learn a lesson from Nehemiah. Instead of running in the face of discouragement, I must pray and work harder with godly determination.

{Dear Father, I pray to stand firm in my resolve to complete the work you have given to me. Strengthen my tired body. Revive my discouraged heart. I pray that your word dwells in me and that I trust your promises. I pray in the name of Jesus. Amen.}

Digging Deeper

- Read **Nehemiah 1:1 – 4:23**. Use a modern translation or a commentary to get an understanding of what
is happening in this passage. Find a verse to keep
before you today, to help you stand encouraged.
- Tell of a time when you felt discouraged about your
food plan, weight loss, body image, etc. Who helped
you the most, through your discouragement?
- Who, in your life today, is like Sanballet and Tobiah?
The Bible says that we are to pray for our enemies.
Are you praying for these discouragers daily?

DAY 24

There is a time for everything, and a season for every activity under heaven. Ecclesiastes 3:1

GOD'S TIMING

When my prayers are not answered "yes," the devil would like me to believe that God doesn't care about me. The truth is that God cares about me deeply. He loves me and His heart hears my prayers. He sees the big picture and I can be certain that His "no" is for my greatest good.

God's "no" gives me an opportunity to practice patience and perseverance. Both of these things help me to develop character. Quite often, it's not that God isn't going to give me what I have requested; it's that my timing is off. God has an eternal agenda, and this means that I might have to experience "not getting my way" as He unfolds His perfect plan.

{Dear Father, thank you for loving me. Thank you for your perfect plan for my life. I pray to grow in trust and patience as you unfold your perfect plan for this day. I pray this in the name of Jesus. Amen.}

Digging Deeper

- Read **Ecclesiastes 3:1-8**. Which verse speaks to you regarding the past 24 hours?
- Tell of a time when God's "no" turned out to be a blessing in disguise.
- How is your God-honoring plan of eating today? How does this fit into God's plan for this season in your life?

DAY 25

We are therefore Christ's ambassadors, as though God were making his appeal through us. We implore you on Christ's behalf: Be reconciled to God.
2 Corinthians 5:20

AN AMBASSADOR FOR CHRIST

One of the worse things about compulsive overeating was how I felt about myself. I hated what I did with the food in secret. It not only showed up as fat on my body, but it also showed up as sadness on my face. More often than not, people would ask me, "What's wrong?" even when I worked hard to cover my deep inner despair. People were not drawn to me. Many times, my countenance drove them away.

As a Christian, I am called to be an ambassador for Christ. Therefore, compulsive overeating is not within God's will for my life. The Bible says in 1 Thessalonians 5:16 to be joyful always.

God calls me at all times, in the power of Jesus, to delight in Him. This delight is the true meaning of joy. When I am joyful, others find me pleasing to be around.

It used to be that I argued and frowned a lot. Now I notice that I'm friendlier—I even smile at strangers. It's something about having God's joy in my heart that causes a peace both inside and out. People are drawn to this peace, and my prayer is I can draw them to Jesus.

{Dear Father, I am so, so grateful for my salvation. I pray that others will come to know you through the joy they see in me. Please make me a godly witness for Jesus' sake. Amen.}

Digging Deeper

- Read **2 Corinthians 5:19-21.** Underline words and phrases that speak to your heart. Look up the definitions of key words. Write a paraphrase of this passage and make a plan to put God's message into this day.
- Write a paragraph or two about how compulsive overeating hurts one's witness for Jesus. Are you still trying to rationalize your compulsive overeating?
- Who have you shared the gospel with lately? What have you been doing to help them to keep growing in Christ?

DAY 26

*How, then, can they call on the one they have not believed
in? And how can they believe in the one of whom they
have not heard? And how can they hear without someone
preaching to them? And how can they preach unless they
are sent? As it is written, "How beautiful are the feet of
those who bring good news!"*
Romans 10:14,15

BEAUTIFUL FEET

Quite a few times, Christians have spoken to me about
having trouble knowing their role in the 12-step rooms. I
share my story: I did not know the Lord when I came into the
rooms. I got abstinent, and as an effort to grow spiritually,
I began seeking a deeper relationship with God as I understood Him.

This seeking eventually brought me to the foot of the
cross. I saw that my addiction was a sin issue and I could do
nothing on my own to fix it. I learned that God in His mercy
had provided a way for my sin issue to be reconciled.

I learned that eternal life could only be obtained through
God's Son, Jesus Christ. I could never work enough steps,
do enough inventories, or make enough amends to ever wash
away my sins. Only the blood of Jesus could.

I put my total trust in Jesus for forgiveness and eternal
life, and I was born again. My eyes became open to a lot of
things in the rooms that I hadn't noticed before. For a while,
I was confused about my role.

I talked to God about it. (I still talk to God about it.)
Today, I understand that my role is to bring the Good News
to the myriad of seekers that populate the 12-step rooms. My
experience, strength, and hope is that Jesus is the answer.

I am called to be a "fisher of men." I am called to share the hope that I have been given with gentleness and respect. My God has given me a mission field in my own backyard. As I grow in my skill of staying abstinent, no matter what, He allows me to compassionately minister to others in the rooms.

{Dear Father, as I hear others share in the rooms, I pray for the willingness and strength to intercede for the things I hear. Give me a deep compassion to encourage those who are weak and to pray for those who are lost. I pray in the name of Jesus. Amen.}

Digging Deeper

- Read **Romans 10:14,15.** Underline words and phrases that speak to your heart. Make a plan to put God's message into this day.
- List at least five unsaved people that you will encounter this week. Have you prayed that the Lord will use you today to draw them to you?
- What are your experiences and thoughts about Christians in the 12-step rooms?

DAY 27

*Praise be to the God and Father of our Lord Jesus Christ,
the Father of compassion and the God of all comfort,
who comforts us in all our troubles, so that we can
comfort those in any trouble with the comfort we
ourselves have received from God.*
2 Corinthians 1:3,4

COMFORTING OTHERS

Whenever I was topping the scales from being out of control with the food again, the last thing I wanted to hear was admonishments from well-meaning friends. I knew better than they that I was jeopardizing my health. I *knew* that I would feel much better about myself if I would "just lose some weight."

They had no idea how beat up I was already feeling. They couldn't see how I longed to have someone come beside me with compassion and understanding. Instead of pointing out my failures, I needed someone who had failed in the same way I was failing but was presently winning the battle. I needed people to stand with me in the gap and not just point it out.

God sent people like that to me. They taught me the skill of weighing and measuring my food without exception, no matter what. They spoke in the first person—sharing their experience, strength, and hope. They told me that "God was doing for them what they could not do for themselves." God used them to comfort me in the same way that He had comforted them.

As a Christian, I have been equipped to show compassion because my God is compassionate and His Spirit lives within me. I am not called to analyze and criticize my friends. Instead, I need to remember how the Lord rescued me when

I was where they presently are. As I lovingly share how I was shown a way out of my difficulty, I find that I am being used by God to comfort others.

{Dear Father, I pray not to add to the burdens of others with accusations and speculations in the midst of their trials. Let me remember how you comforted me, and empower me to share from that source alone. I pray this in the name of Jesus. Amen.}

Digging Deeper

- Read **2 Corinthians 1:2-4**. Underline words and phrases that speak to your heart. Look up the definitions of key words. Write a paraphrase of this passage and make a plan to put God's message into this day.
- List the people who were true friends to you through your battles of compulsive overeating. How did they help you? What can you learn from their experience, strength, and hope? Do you presently have the willingness to apply these lessons? Are you willing to ask God for the willingness?
- This would be a good time to read the book of Job. Pay special attention to his friends. Are you this type of friend? Did their words bring comfort to him?

DAY 28

*Late in the afternoon the Twelve came to him and said,
"Send the crowd away so they can go to the surrounding
villages and countryside and find food and lodging,
because we are in a remote place here." He replied,
"You give them something to eat."*
Luke 9:12-13a

YOU GIVE THEM SOMETHING TO EAT

I knew well the person on the other end of the phone. I could tell from her voice that she was on the edge. She was progressing in her recovery, but I could tell that tonight she was shaky. I was trying hard to meet a deadline, but I knew she needed to talk.

I prayed and the Lord gave me the willingness and the strength to listen to her pain. She was lonely. She was getting discouraged. I asked her if she had had any time alone with the Lord. She said that she had prayed the night before, but when I probed a little bit more, she admitted that it was just a short prayer for help.

I shared with her that it always helped me to get my Bible out, read a passage, and then pray that same passage. I also reminded her that if she was not willing, she could ask the Lord to give her the willingness that she needed.

Then the conviction came as I remembered the story of the "Feeding of the Five Thousand": *The apostles were tired. The crowd was large. It was late and when the Twelve asked Jesus to send the crowd away so that they could find food, Jesus replied, "You give them something to eat."*

She was calling me. She knew, from past conversations, what needed to be done, but she was too weak to do it at the moment. I prayed again, and the Lord heard my prayer.

Together we prayed, read a psalm together, talked, and prayed some more. When we ended our conversation and I was back doing the work before me, I felt a deep glow inside. She had been strengthened, and I had been blessed. God is so, so good.

{Dear Father, I forget so quickly that it's not about me. It's about You! You are mighty and powerful and nothing is impossible with You. I pray to abandon even the thought that I can help another in my own strength. I pray in the name of Jesus. Amen.}

Digging Deeper

- Read the story of the "Feeding of the Five Thousand" found in **Luke 9:10-17**. Write down seven things that you remember from the reading. What lessons might God be trying to teach you in your present circumstances?
- How hospitable are you? Do you provide food for others? Why or why not? Do you provide spiritual food for others? Why or why not?
- Share about a time when you were blessed by giving unselfishly to another.

DAY 29

We are hard pressed on every side, but not crushed;
perplexed, but not in despair; persecuted, but not
abandoned; struck down, but not destroyed.
We always carry around in our body the death of Jesus,
so that the life of Jesus may also be revealed in our body.
2 Corinthians 4:8-10

NOT IN DESPAIR

Compulsive overeating was depressing. Near the end of my overeating career, stuffing myself was no longer fun. I had had too many mornings after full of despair and self-loathing, to find any enjoyment after the first few compulsive bites. Many times, though, I still took the bites, and without fail, I eventually hated myself for doing so.

It has been said that nothing tastes as good as abstinence feels. This was certainly my experience in my first few years of abstinence. I felt better before it even showed physically. Later, I could notice that I was getting smaller and this, too, made me feel great. It was wonderful to wake up with hope and energy for the day.

For a while, I thought that abstinence alone was the answer to my despair. It took a while to realize that being disciplined and successful with my food drew others to me. Some thought that I could walk on water. Others desired to see "signs and wonders." In my own strength, I lacked the power to meet the expectations of a flourishing life. I needed something more.

In Philippians 3:10, Paul wrote, "I want to know Christ and the power of His resurrection." I came to understand that the power that resurrected Jesus from the dead was the power that I needed to live my life abstinent, helpful, and free.

Because Jesus is my Lord, I don't ever have to fear the pressures of life today. He keeps me from being crushed. He has given me a legacy of eternal hope, and nothing can destroy me and keep me down.

{Dear Father, thank you for giving me a way to be fruitful and having a meaningful life. I pray to remember that without Jesus I can do nothing. Without Him, I will return to hopelessness and despair. Keep me close to Jesus. I pray this in His holy name. Amen.}

Digging Deeper

- Read **2 Corinthians 4:1-18**. In this chapter are several beautiful, strengthening verses. Prayerfully consider committing one or more of these to memory today.
- How long has it been since you experience the hopelessness and despair brought on by compulsive overeating? Have you thanked God for your abstinence? If you are still struggling with the food, have you continued to ask for the willingness and strength again and again and again to abstain?
- Is Jesus your Lord and Savior? What, exactly, does this mean to you today?

DAY 30

Be self-controlled and alert. Your enemy the devil prowls around like a roaring lion looking for someone to devour.
1 Peter 5:8

DOING PUSH-UPS

As long as I have breath, I will have to deal with the devil trying to bring me down. In fact, the devil seems to love it best when he cannot only hurt me, but also those who I shepherd. He strives for the domino effect—topple the one in the lead and the rest will be knocked over as well.

There is a saying in the 12-step rooms that as a person is in a meeting working on recovery, the disease is right outside the door doing push-ups. Indeed, some of my worst attacks came right after major successes in maintaining my abstinence.

I have seen it happen with others as well. A person comes in. They work to recover. They get several months behind them. They begin sponsoring others. They forget that they are never beyond being tempted to return to former ways. They have a slip, and many who looked up to them fall by the wayside, too.

As a Christian, I am called to be self-controlled and alert. As I mature to positions of leadership, I must especially be on guard. The devil hasn't gone anywhere. In fact, he is planning a major defensive. Nevertheless, I need not turn back in fear. Jesus is my sure and present help. As I abide in Him daily, I can stand firm and be victorious.

{Dear Father, I pray not to be surprised by temptation. Please give me the willingness and strength to keep vigilant. Keep me standing strong when temptation comes. I pray to

*maintain the disciplines that help to build me up in the faith.
In the name of Jesus, I pray. Amen.}*

Digging Deeper

- Read **1 Peter 5:7-11**. Underline words and phrases
  that speak to your heart. Look up the definitions of
  key words. Write a paraphrase of this passage and
  make a plan to put God's message into this day.
- Have you been careless in your abstinence lately?
  Are you maintaining the vigilance that you once
  had when you were first counting days? Have you
  forgotten the weakness of your flesh regarding
  compulsive overeating?
- How knowledgeable are you concerning the global
  persecution of Christians? Are you willing to learn
  more about this? How might this knowledge help
  your faith?

DAY 31

All Scripture is God-breathed and is useful for teaching,
rebuking, correcting and training in righteousness,
so that the man of God may be thoroughly equipped
for every good work.
2 Timothy 3:16, 17

THOROUGHLY EQUIPPED

About four or five years ago, I asked members of a Bible study to pray that I would have the willingness and strength to begin scripture memory. I was convinced that knowing scripture by heart was important, but I just couldn't seem to do it. God answered that prayer, and scripture memory is now a very essential part of my daily quiet time.

Over the years, I have used different techniques for the actual memorization phase. I have written the verse over and over. I have memorized phrase by phrase. I have memorized by making up a song with the words of the verse. I have even said the verse rhythmically aloud as I marched around the room, which seems to work well with long passages. I do whatever it takes.

Once I have memorized the verse, I must make up my mind to keep it in my memory through daily review. I have prayed, and God has given me the willingness to spend 3 to 7 minutes a day to review verses that I have memorized.

I review by using little flash cards. I find a copy of the verse online, print it out, and paste it on the back of an old business card. On the front of the card I write the first three or so words of the verse. On most days, I review these myself. Every once and awhile, though, I get my teenage son to test me. He gives me the three-word prompt. I tell him the "address" and repeat the verse. I don't need to tell you how much of a kick he gets when he has to correct me! The neat thing, though, is that we both benefit. As he has helped me to review the verses I've watched that, he, too, has learned verses.

I encourage you to ask God to give you the willingness to be diligent in learning and reviewing scripture on a consistent basis. The verse you study might not just keep you going, but it could also equip countless others as you share what you are learning.

{Dear Father, I pray for the willingness and strength to hide your word in my heart today. Thank you for your word, which is truly powerful and active in my life. I pray and give thanks in the name of Jesus. Amen.}

Digging Deeper

- Read **2 Timothy 3:14-17.** Underline words and phrases that speak to your heart. Look up the definitions of key words. Write a paraphrase of this passage and make a plan to put God's message into this day.
- Having good, clean abstinence requires that we have certain tools to keep us "thoroughly equipped." What are these tools for you? Have they changed any since your beginning days of abstinence? Is this good or bad?
- Is Bible memory a part of your daily quiet time? Have you talked to God about this? Have you tried asking others to pray for you about this?

DAY 32

You will keep in perfect peace him whose mind is steadfast, because he trusts in you. Trust in the LORD forever, for the LORD, the LORD, is the Rock eternal.
Isaiah 26:3,4

A STEADFAST MIND

When I was first getting abstinent, I learned the importance of focusing on the right things. One of the first lessons toward doing this was keeping my concerns within the present 24 hours. I can remember asking myself, "How can I stay abstinent TODAY?" It didn't matter that a dinner party was going to happen tomorrow. It didn't matter that a car trip was being planned for next week. It didn't matter that a friend's wedding was a month away. I didn't know exactly how I was going to stay abstinent for any of those things, but it didn't matter. What mattered was staying abstinent in the present 24 hours. I would paraphrase what I had heard on an AA tape: "Today is the day I don't eat!"

In my Christian life, keeping the right focus is just as important. Many things come up for which I don't have ready solutions. The unknown threatens to rob me of my peace of mind. I can start to feel anxious, overwhelmed, and depressed. I am reminded that when it comes to my feelings, I "reap what I sow." If I sow thoughts that are not fitting for one who is redeemed, eventually my feelings will be "off".

Because I belong to Jesus, peace is a promise. God will keep me in a deep and abiding peace as I let my mind keep a steady course to things that will brings glory to His name. When my feelings are "off," the question becomes, "What lie am I believing?" If I replace it with the truth of God's word, my thinking and eventually my feelings will get back on track.

It's all about Jesus. Everything I do has to be all about Him. Everything I think has to be about living the way that He has laid out for me to live. There are troubles in this world, but I can take heart because He has overcome the world! (John 14:33)

{Dear Father, I pray to stay alert. Give me the willingness to take every thought captive to make it obedient to Your word. Keep my mind steadfast to Your truth. I pray this in Jesus' name. Amen.}

Digging Deeper

- Read **Isaiah 26:3-4** in at least three versions of the Bible. Which version speaks strongest to your heart? Will you ask for the willingness and strength to work on Bible memory today?
- What thoughts most threaten your abstinence? How do you deal with this?
- What does trusting the Lord mean to you? What things are causing you to trust the Lord more?

DAY 33

*Surely He has borne our griefs and carried our sorrows;
Yet we esteemed Him stricken, smitten by God, and
afflicted. But He was wounded for our transgressions, He
was bruised for our iniquities; The chastisement for our
peace was upon Him, and by His stripes we are healed.*
Isaiah 53:4-5

MISUNDERSTANDING

Sometimes when people see me weighing and measuring my food, they view it as a hardship. Some have even said with pity, "It's a shame that you just can't let go and 'have fun' once in a while." A part of me wants to get huffy and say, "You just don't get it!" But God reminds me that there was time when I just "didn't get it" either. Once, like them, I saw abstinence as a restriction. Today, by the grace of God, I know it as a gift. I misunderstood. God opened my eyes.

Jesus was misunderstood. As He walked the road to Calvary, many watched along the way. Here was one who healed the sick and raised the dead. Here was one who said that He was one with God, yet it made no sense to them what they were presently seeing. This "man" had now been beaten to the point of death. He was disfigured and so weakened that another man had to carry his cross. To them, Jesus appeared to be forgotten by God.

I misunderstood, Jesus, too. I had heard the story of Jesus' crucifixion for years, yet I never knew in my heart what it had to do with me personally. I had not come to terms with my own, private sin nature, let alone my powerlessness to fix it. I knew I wasn't perfect, but, I thought, I was WAY better than most. They needed a savior, not me. I wasn't *that* bad.

I know Jesus today as God's gift to me. I never could have fixed my misunderstanding of Jesus by myself. In His mercy, God gave me the faith to embrace the Good News. If you are reading this today and are still baffled by Jesus, I challenge you to ask God to give you the faith to see the truth about Him. He really wants you to understand.

{Dear Jesus, for so many years I was your enemy. I thought I didn't need you. I thought I was good enough for God, your Father, just as I was. Thank you for loving me and saving me—even when I didn't love you. I want to be a better witness, for Your sake. Teach me to share the Good News from a place of deep gratitude for what You did for me. It's in Your name that I pray. Amen.}

Digging Deeper

- Read **Isaiah 53:4,5**. Write down your thoughts about this passage.
- Take time to read about Saul in **Acts 9:1-19**. Are you presently like Saul had been? Are you trying to work for God without a relationship with Jesus?
- How do you act when others disapprove of your abstinence? Have you talked to the Lord about it?

DAY 34

As iron sharpens iron, so one man sharpens another.
Proverbs 27:17

SPONSORSHIP

It took quite some years in the 12-step rooms before I had enough humility to let a sponsor truly guide me. My pride, coupled with memories of times when people had disappointed me, made me leery of sponsorship. I had little confidence that anyone could teach me anything. It took the failure of trying to control my overeating "my way" to be willing to humbly follow the directions of a sponsor.

The person who guided me through my first 90 days of this present abstinence was far from my perfect ideal of a sponsor. Our personalities and backgrounds were on opposite ends of the spectrum. If I had not been so desperate, I might have gone "sponsor shopping" for someone more like me. I thank God, today, that I WAS so desperate. The year that I worked with that original sponsor taught me, first hand, the wisdom of "principles before personalities." When it came to abstinence, she was clean, clear, and committed. She had the willingness to make the time daily to teach me how to "weigh and measure without exception, no matter what." Regarding sponsorship, this was more than enough.

From her example, I learned the importance of keeping an attitude of gratitude for my abstinence. From her, I learned that the best insurance against that "first compulsive bite" was giving away what was so freely given to me. When I reached my 90 days, she taught me not to fear being a sponsor. The skills that she had passed on to me became sharpened as I passed them along to others. As I helped others to appreciate clean and committed abstinence, I grew stronger in my own appreciation.

I thank God for many years of back-to-back abstinence. I thank God for those who have sponsored me. I thank God for the ones that I have had the privilege to sponsor. Sponsorship reminds me that it is indeed a "we" program.

{Dear Father, thank you for this day of abstinence. Thank you for the skills that you have provided and the teachers you have sent to train me. I pray that I am willing to be there for others as others have been there for me. I pray in the name of Jesus. Amen.}

Digging Deeper

- Sponsorship requires humility from both sides. Read **Philippians 2:1-11**. List the things that you learn about humility from Jesus' example.
- Write about the sponsors you have had in the program. What did you learn from each of them?
- Are you sponsoring others? If not, why not? What are some of the lessons you have learned as a result of sponsoring others?

DAY 35

In your hearts set apart Christ as Lord. Always be prepared to give an answer to everyone who asks you to give the reason for the hope that you have. But do this with gentleness and respect.
1 Peter 3:15

SO GRATEFUL

Jesus has done a wonderful thing in me. He changed my heart. He made me brand new. When I think about how awesome this is, I am filled with such gratitude. I am like the man who was possessed by many demons. When Jesus drove the demons from him, others found him "clothed and in his right mind." Like him, I wanted to leave everything behind me, but He sent me back home to tell others how much God has done for me. (Luke 8:26-39)

There have been times when I have tried to go out to tell others and I have blown it. I have forgotten to "set apart Christ as Lord." Or, I haven't done my homework. Or, (and this is a BIG one), I have failed to share the gospel with "gentleness and respect."

When I treat people with impatience and arrogance, I am forgetting where I came from and how Jesus found me. I cannot afford to forget. My ability to witness well for Jesus is so dependent upon remembering Jesus' rescue of me. *He lifted me out of the slimy pit, out of the mud and mire; he set my feet on a rock and gave me a firm place to stand. He put a new song in my mouth, a hymn of praise to our God. Many will see and fear and put their trust in the LORD.* (Psalm 40:2,3)

{Dear Father, I pray to keep a grateful heart. You have given me so very much. I want to be like Jesus. I want to draw others to you, in Jesus' name. Amen.}

Digging Deeper

- Read **Luke 8:29-39**. Retell the story in your own words. What can you learn about gratitude from this story?
- Are you grateful for your abstinence? How is this gratitude shown in your witness?
- Use your concordance to find at least three verses on the subject of gratitude. Write down these verses. Ask God for the willingness to memorize one of these verses.

DAY 36

When this had dawned on him, he went to the house of Mary the mother of John, also called Mark, where many people had gathered and were praying.
Acts 12:12

SOMEBODY'S PRAYING ME THROUGH

There is a song sung by Allen Asbury that almost brings me to tears each time that I hear it. It's entitled "Somebody's Praying Me Through." The first verse of the song reads like this: *Pressing over me like a big blue sky. I know someone has me on their heart tonight. Thats why I know it's gonna be alright. 'Cause... somebody's praying me through. Somebody's praying me through.* [1]

I was not alone when I look back over some of life's worse situations. I know that I got through them only because of the prayers of the saints. I didn't always know who the prayer warrior was, but oh, was I so grateful for their obedience!

In the twelfth chapter of Acts, there lies a powerful example of how prayer can break through a seemingly impossible situation: The early church is going through tremendous persecution. Peter is in jail waiting for his trial before King Herod. James, another one of the apostles, had been arrested before Peter, and Herod had put him to death. For Peter, it just seems like a matter of time before he meets the same end.

Despite death hanging over his head, Peter is able to sleep. Looking at verse 5 in this chapter is the reason why Peter is able to have such peace in a terrible situation: *So Peter was kept in prison, but the church was earnestly praying to God for him.*

The miracle continues. Despite the fact that Peter is chained and guard heavily, an angel is able to come to his rescue and free him. Peter then walks to the place where his brethren are praying; they are astonished and, I'm certain, filled with joy unthinkable at this incredible miracle!

{Dear Father, your love for me is amazing! Thank you for the body of Christ. Thank you for my sisters and brothers who pray faithfully on my behalf. I pray to be a faithful prayer warrior, too. It's in Jesus' name that I pray. Amen.}

Digging Deeper

- Read **Act 12: 1-19**. Write down seven things that you remember from the reading. What lessons might God be trying to teach you in your present circumstances?
- Do you have people who faithfully pray for your abstinence? Do you earnestly pray for the abstinence of your brothers and sisters in the rooms? If not, might God be calling you to begin today?
- Tell of a time when you later looked back and could say, "Somebody's praying me through."

DAY 37

"Martha, Martha," the Lord answered, "you are worried and upset about many things, but only one thing is needed. Mary has chosen what is better, and it will not be taken away from her."
Luke 10:41-42

JESUS FIRST

In the gospel of Luke 10:38-42, Jesus visits the home of dear friends and sisters, Martha and Mary. On this particular visit, Martha was so concerned with getting things ready for Jesus' visit that she became bothered and quite grouchy. Martha went to Jesus saying, "Lord, don't you care that my sister has left me to do the work by myself? Tell her to help me!"

Jesus in His wisdom reminded Martha of "first things first." He, the living God, was present with them. Preparations needed to cease. Now was the time for Martha to sit at the feet of the Lord, as Mary was doing.

More times than I care to remember have been characterized by much anxiety and worry about details. Many opportunities to experience the love of Jesus have been missed in too much movement. As a Christian, I am called to make My Lord my highest priority. Worry results when I fail to do this. Jesus is calling me to sit at His feet in order to receive what is best.

{Dear Father, you have given me important things to do—I am to know Jesus and to make Him known. I can do neither of these things in my own strength. I pray to be teachable. I pray to sit at the feet of your Son with a heart longing to learn. I pray this in the name of Jesus. Amen.}

Digging Deeper

- Read **Luke 10:38-42**. Write down seven things that you remember from the reading. What lessons might God be trying to teach you in your present circumstances?
- It's possible to be a "Martha" when it comes to preparing abstinent meals. Has having a "10" meal become your most important consideration at mealtime? Do you ever think of a shared eating experience as an opportunity to witness? When was the last time you reminded yourself that there was another meal coming? Have you ever opted for a simpler meal in order to have a better time of fellowship with another?
- When was the last time you, like Mary, sat at the feet of Jesus? What did He teach you? How is His lesson affecting your behavior today?

DAY 38

Then it goes and takes with it seven other spirits more wicked than itself, and they go in and live there. And the final condition of that man is worse than the first. That is how it will be with this wicked generation.
Matthew 12:45

RELAPSE

Relapse is horrible. My last one lasted two years. The memory of how far it brought me down gets me on my knees the first thing in the morning. I thank God for the abstinence of the day before. I pray for the present day's abstinence.

In relapse, I could find no peace. There was no escaping the knowledge that I had once experienced a better way. Overeating was anything but fun in relapse. At best, it was just the means to a short-lived blackout.

Maintaining my abstinence requires that I continue to grow spiritually. One of my devotions reminds me that just as my physical body requires water and the right foods, my walk with God requires careful tending. There is much around me that threatens to turn my head and my heart in the wrong direction. By myself, on my own, I can easily forget to keep God number one.

Without a Christian community, I can lose sight of the fact that God's will for me is not a mystery. The Holy Spirit lives in me, and the Scripture testifies to the truth that has been written in my heart. What a truly wonderful thing to have a community of believers who know my disease and share my recovery. God is good, very good!

{Father, I pray never to relapse again. Thank you for the body of Christ who prays for me and supports me. Thank you for your beautiful provision. In Jesus' name, I pray. Amen.}

Digging Deeper

- Read **Matthew 12:43-45.** Underline words and phrases that speak to your heart. Look up the definitions of key words. Write a paraphrase of this passage and make a plan to put God's message into this day.
- Have you ever relapsed? What safeguards do you presently have in place against a relapse today?
- How seriously do you hide the word of God in your heart? What have you learned about Bible study's role in your recovery?

DAY 39

Finally, brothers, whatever is true, whatever is noble,
whatever is right, whatever is pure, whatever is lovely,
whatever is admirable—if anything is excellent or
praiseworthy—think about such things.
Philippians 4:8

AVOIDING SABOTAGE

I have learned the importance of not allowing my mind to dwell on food in ways that could trigger my obsession. This doesn't mean that I don't totally enjoy the look, taste, and smell of my meal when it is before me and I am ready to eat. Not obsessing over the food means that when it is not a mealtime, I need to fill my mind with other things.

I was taught that when it comes to eating, I not only have a compulsive disease, but I also have obsessive one. This is the logic of writing down my meals and calling them in—it cuts down on the possibility of getting into food fantasizing. Outside of a mealtime, I learned that thinking longingly about the look, taste, or smell of even abstinent food would make me hungry. I knew that before long I would feel deprived and victimized if I allowed myself to fantasize. And before long, I would get angry that I could not "indulge" like everyone else in the world. And before long I would be knee deep in "stinking' thinkin'," which would have me believing that I "deserved" to have whatever I craved. Then the binge would begin...again.

The Bible teaches that not only am I to scrutinize my thoughts (2 Corinthians 10:5), but I am also to focus my thinking (Philippians 4:8). The evil one would like to have me believe that what is good is actually bad and what is bad is actually good. There have been times when I have been in the midst of blessings, and wrong thinking had me believing that I had been cursed.

Each day, I can be transformed by the renewing of my mind (Romans 12:2). God is so good to provide His holy word, the Bible. Through it, I learn His will and mature in my faith. I learn to side step the pitfalls that would sabotage my abstinence and my keeping in step with the Spirit.

{Dear Father, keep me from the devil's strongholds. Convict me when my thinking is off. Help me to grow in the knowledge and love of the Lord Jesus. I pray this in His holy name. Amen.}

Digging Deeper

- Read **Philippians 4:4-9**. Underline words and phrases that speak to your heart. Look up the definitions of key words. Write a paraphrase of this passage and make a plan to put God's message into this day.
- What type of thinking has the potential of sabotaging your abstinence? How do you safeguard your mind against it?
- **Philippians 4** has many verses that could strengthen your heart. Pray for the willingness and strength now to chose one to memorize.

DAY 40

Your word is a lamp to my feet and a light for my path.
Psalm 119:105

GOD'S LOVE LETTER

Before I was born again, the Bible did not mean that much to me. I had never been in a Bible study. I had never read the Bible from cover to cover. Most of it made no sense to me.

Later, I heard it said that the reason the Bible made no sense was because I was reading someone else's mail. The Bible is God's love letter to His children. I didn't become God's child until I was saved through the blood of Jesus.

The moment that I accepted Jesus as my Lord and Savior, his Spirit was poured out into my heart. Now as I read the scripture, this Spirit gives me understanding. I know first hand that "the word of God is living and active. Sharper than any double edged sword." (Hebrews 4:12)

Because of the Bible, I have wisdom and power in my life that is beyond what I even knew. God is truly good and wonderful.

{Thank you, Father, for your will is no longer a mystery. Each time that I study and apply your word, your will becomes clearer and clearer. Thank you for training and equipping me. I pray to keep growing in my love for the Lord Jesus Christ. I give you thanks in His holy name. Amen.}

Digging Deeper

- Read **Psalm 119:105-112**. Underline words and phrases that speak to your heart. Look up the definitions of key words. Write a paraphrase of this passage and make a plan to put God's message into this day.
- When did you come to know the Lord Jesus as your savior? What were the steps that led up to your salvation? What does your abstinence have to do with you being a fruitful Christian?
- Tell of a time when you were baffled and uncertain, and the word of God brought you understanding and direction.

DAY 41

Come to me, all you who are weary and burdened,
and I will give you rest. Take my yoke upon you
and learn from me, for I am gentle and humble in heart,
and you will find rest for your souls. For my yoke
is easy and my burden is light.
Matthew 11:28-30

TIREDNESS VS. WEARINESS

Tiredness in me is the result of physical labor. Weariness is the result of misdirected thinking. My initial response when I don't feel that I have the energy to do the work that needs to be done is "I'm tired." The truth is that quite often it's weariness. I have allowed thoughts of doubt and discouragement to linger in my mind. Before long, I feel burdened and defeated. Sad to say, I have sometimes walked away from godly activities because I have felt "too tired."

Jesus wants me to bind myself to Him before I set out to tackle my daily tasks. As I walk side by side with Him, as a yokefellow, I get a different perspective. It's not about me doing a "new thing" and then asking God for His stamp of approval. On the contrary, as author Henry Blackaby has said that it's all about joining God in His work.

Joining God, as oppose to directing Him, gives my life a whole different focus. I must become smaller, and Jesus must become larger. (see John 3:30) God desires that I become more like Jesus. I am called to grow in gentleness and in my willingness to learn.

Walking side by side with Jesus is not burdensome. He loves me, and even in hard times, I am powerfully sustained by His peace.

{Thank you, Father, for I am never alone. Jesus is with me in all that You call me to do. Thank you for loving me so much. Thank you for giving me Jesus. It's in His name that I pray. Amen.}

Digging Deeper

- Read **Matthew 11:27-30.** Write down seven things that God might be trying to teach you in this passage.
- How is your abstinence feeling lately? Do you see it as a blessing or a curse?
- Write out three verses of scripture that help you to experience God's place of rest. Which is your favorite and why?

DAY 42

*The fear of the LORD is the beginning of knowledge,
but fools despise wisdom and discipline. Listen, my son,
to your father's instruction
and do not forsake your mother's teaching.*
Proverbs 1:7-8

EMBRACING CORRECTION

My flesh hates being told what to do. I realize this when-ever my sponsor has to correct me. My heart knows that she is passing on guidelines with the food that she herself follows. The "voices of the evil one," nonetheless, try to convince me that she is trying to destroy my "fun."

Sponsoring others helps me to see how foolish this reac-tion is. I want the best for my sponsees. I want them to grow in their abstinence. I want them to grow to be all that God desires for them to be. When I tell them "No" or correct a misstep, I do it because I care. How foolish it is to think that my sponsor does not want the same for me!

Growing in faith requires that I learn to rise above feel-ings of hate for correction. God provides correction so that I can stay on the straight and narrow. I am given feedback that teaches me how to avoid future mistakes.

I am learning to pray when I have to be disciplined. I ask God to take away the thoughts that are the lies of the evil one. I seek to fill my thinking with the truth of God.

Only a loving God can make such a thoughtful provi-sion. Being disciplined shows God's mindfulness. I am His child, by the blood of Jesus. I am cared about and greatly loved. Correction is a sign of this love.

{Dear Father, thank you that you care enough about me to teach me and correct me. Please strengthen my faith. Please grow me up so that I might embrace the discipline that you provide. I pray this in the name of Jesus. Amen.}

Digging Deeper

- Read **Proverbs 1:1-33**. If possible, find a modern translation of this Proverb. List the ways that God might be speaking to you personally through this passage.
- How is your present relationship with your sponsor? Do you trust her love and care for you? If not, have you prayed to the Lord about this?
- Use a Bible search engine such as Biblegateway.com to find several verses concerning discipline. Ask God for the willingness to memorize one of these verses.

DAY 43

*Be still in the presence of the LORD, and wait patiently
for him to act. Don't worry about evil people who prosper
or fret about their wicked schemes.*
Psalm 37:7 (NLT)

WHEN LIFE SEEMS UNFAIR

When evil seems to be getting the upper hand in the world around me, I am learning not to worry but to pray and turn to God's word. It is a "given" that there will be times when the wicked will prosper and those who are trying to please the Lord will suffer. We live in a fallen world, and sin brings pain—even to innocent people.

The Holy Spirit is helping me to look beyond the outer surface of things. This is God's world. He is not asleep on the job. He knows what is "going down," and in

His time, divine justice will be shown. God's word reminds me that my destiny as a believer is eternal joy with God. It's foolish for me to envy the lost. Instead, I am called to pray for their salvation.

God has prepared a wonderful place for me. I pray to trust the Lord even when life is "stinky." I pray to be loyal in my praise and thanksgiving at all times, "no matter what!"

{Dear Father, forgive me for the times when I have pouted and complained about life. You have given me salvation, which is priceless. I pray to grow in trust and obedience to your Word. In Jesus' name I pray. Amen.}

Digging Deeper

- Read **Psalm 37:1-11**. If possible, find a modern translation of this passage. List the ways that God might be speaking to you personally.
- Have you made a list, lately, of people of whom you are "out of step"? Are you praying for reconciliation in these relationships? Are resentment and unforgiveness trying to make a comeback in your heart?
- If someone asked you, "Do you trust in the Lord?", how would you answer them? What would be the reasons behind your answer?

DAY 44

But Samuel replied, "What is more pleasing to the LORD:
your burnt offerings and sacrifices or your obedience
to his voice? Obedience is far better than sacrifice.
Listening to him is much better than offering the fat of
rams. Rebellion is as bad as the sin of witchcraft, and
stubbornness is as bad as worshiping idols.
1 Samuel 15:22,23a

OBEDIENCE IS BETTER

I love getting gifts from my children. I feel cherished, remembered and astounded by their creativity. Nevertheless, if it ever came down to a choice, I would rather that my children follow my directions than shower me with treasures.

I know that God feels the same way about me. I can boast of great works and plenteous service for God, but if I have disobeyed Him, I have displeased Him.

In 1 Samuel 15:1-23, Saul, the King of Israel, learns this the hard way. He does some of the things that God asks, but he chooses to do his will and rationalizes his transgressions. As a result, it becomes clear that God can no longer use Saul as a leader and he is eventually replaced by David.

Obedience is willingly yielding to the control of another. Obedience means following the complete directions and not just the parts that are pleasing. Partial obedience is just a fancy name for disobedience.

I show that I love God when I do the things that He asks me to do. Whenever I sense resistance, I am learning to pray. God is such a gracious God. He can even make me willing to obey Him. All I need to do is to ask.

{Dear Father, thank you for placing your Spirit in me. I have surrendered my will to you through the acceptance of Jesus as my Lord and Savior, and you have blessed me mightily. Thank you, thank you, thank you!}

Digging Deeper

- Read **1 Samuel 15:1-23**. Write down as many things as you can remember from the reading. What are the lessons there for you?
- What role does obedience play in maintaining your abstinence?
- Use a concordance to find at least three verses on obedience. Chose one to do a verse study: underline and define key words, paraphrase, make a plan for application.

DAY 45

*For it is by grace you have been saved, through faith —
and this not from yourselves, it is the gift of God —
not by works, so that no one can boast.*
Ephesians 2:8,9

WERE IT NOT FOR GRACE

Larnell Harris sings a song, "Were It Not For Grace." It's one of my favorites because it tells the story of my unsaved life. The words of the chorus reads:

*Were it not for grace, I can tell you where I'd be
Wandering down some pointless road to nowhere
With my salvation up to me.
I know how that would go
The battles I would face
Forever running, but losing the race
Were it not for grace.*

Before receiving Jesus as my Lord and savior, I had this deep, deep yearning for purpose and place. I did not know it, but I was seeking to have an intimate relationship with God. Up until this time, knowing God was about performing good works, in the hopes of gaining approval. There were times when I felt His love, but these times were often fleeting. I had no idea how to please God all of the time.

Jesus is a God-given gift (John 3:16). He became the supreme sacrifice so that I could be reconciled to God eternally. When I received Jesus as my savior and Lord, my peace was made with God. Because I am covered by the blood of Jesus, I am pleasing to God. Jesus is my righteousness. I am eternally grateful.

{Thank you, Father, for sending your Shepherd to save me. Thank you for giving me the faith to accept your gift of love. I give you my praise, with all of my heart, in Jesus' name. Amen.}

Digging Deeper

- Read **Ephesians 2:8-9**. Underline words and phrases that speak to your heart. Look up the definitions of key words. Write a paraphrase of this passage and make a plan to put God's message into this day.
- Do you have a personal relationship with God through His son, Jesus Christ? How would you define grace?
- Is your eating today, God honoring? Have you kept your commitment? Do you have an accountability partner? Are you using the help that God is giving to you?

DAY 46

This is what the LORD says: "Let not the wise man boast
of his wisdom or the strong man boast of his strength or
the rich man boast of his riches, but let him who boasts
boast about this: that he understands and knows me, that
I am the LORD, who exercises kindness,
justice and righteousness on earth,
for in these I delight," declares the LORD.
Jeremiah 9:23,24

GIVING GOD THE GLORY

I have a friend in the rooms who always says that this is a "we" program. Through her sharing I am reminded not to boast about my recovery, but to give God the glory. Indeed, many people have gone before me. Many people are presently walking beside me. Each day, I benefit from their "experience, strength, and hope" which strengthens my resolve to "not eat no matter what!"

As I grow in my faith, I have to avoid spiritual pride. My flesh would have me believing that I have always been able to live my life well. Through God's grace, I can exercise wisdom, strength, and productivity—all gifts from a loving God. I pray to always remember to side step the temptation to take the credit. I could do nothing outside the love of God, which is in Christ Jesus my Lord.

{Dear Father, convict me when I try to steal the honor that is due your name. I pray to remember that it's not about the gift. It's about You, the giver. May I give you praise at all times. I pray in the name of Jesus. Amen.}

Digging Deeper

- Read **Jeremiah 9:23, 24**. Do a study of these verses. Look up the key words, define the words and write a paraphrase of these verses. Write out two actions you can take to help you withstand the temptation to boast.
- Of these gifts—wisdom, strength, or riches, which are you most likely to boast?
- Which of these gifts do you value the most in others? Is there someone that you are making (or have made) a false god? Do you owe them an amend?
- List some of the people in the rooms, who have more time than you. How have they helped you in your abstinence? Have you thanked them lately?

DAY 47

Then Jesus said to his disciples, "If anyone would come after me, he must deny himself and take up his cross and follow me. For whoever wants to save his life will lose it, but whoever loses his life for me will find it.
Matthew 16:24-25

FOR JESUS' SAKE

In the program, service is a wonderful thing. But when I lose my focus of why I serve, I put my abstinence in jeopardy. I learned this the hard way some years before this present abstinence. I was working hard to "carry the message" and "practice the principles," but, somehow, I started looking around me. I compared what I was doing to what I perceived others "not doing." Before long, I became resentful and bitter. I eventually gave into temptation and lost my abstinence.

Serving others is not always easy. This is why I must be clear in my heart as to why I serve. Otherwise, I can become angry, hateful, and HUNGRY!

Jesus left heaven for me. He suffered and died for my sins. His sacrifice on my behalf fills me with such a deep sense of thankfulness. I serve today because I remember Jesus and what He did for me. I am eternally grateful. He is there for me. I want to be there for Him.

{Dear Father, I pray not to be naïve about the work it requires to serve You well. I pray to surrender my desire for heaven-on-earth living. Give me an eternal perspective. Help me to rely on the Holy Spirit for both direction and perseverance as I do the work that You are needing me to do. I pray to fix my eyes on Jesus through both the highs and lows of serving You. Give me strength and courage to persevere with a joyful and loving attitude. I pray this in the name of Jesus. Amen.}

Digging Deeper

- Read **Matthew 16:21-26**. Summarize this passage. What are some of the main themes of this reading? What lessons might you apply in your own life?
- What is your present attitude about serving others in the rooms? What might Jesus say about this?
- Choose a verse from Matthew 16:21-26 to do a verse study. Look up and define the key words. Paraphrase the verse. Write out a plan for yourself to put this verse into action.

DAY 48

Therefore do not let sin reign in your mortal body so that you obey its evil desires. Do not offer the parts of your body to sin, as instruments of wickedness, but rather offer yourselves to God, as those who have been brought from death to life; and offer the parts of your body to him as instruments of righteousness.
Romans 6:12-13

SICK AND TIRED

As long as I saw my overeating as "no big deal", I could not stay abstinent. I had to see past the short-lived pleasure and on to the ugliness. I had to remember the upset stomach, the huge bowel movements, the wasted money, the wasted time, the lying, the hiding, the hating myself, and the merry-go-round of despair and depression. I had to become "sick and tired of being sick and tired."

To overeat would be to offer my body as an instrument for wickedness. Nothing would thrill the devil more than to have me immersed in the food and wasting this precious day. But praise the Lord! I know that I am no longer a slave to sin. I have been redeemed. I desire to labor for the Lord. There is Kingdom work to be done, and I am grateful for the privilege and eager to get started.

{Dear Father, I pray to always see the ugliness of my addiction. I pray to never again be enticed by it's false promises. Draw me closer to Jesus. I want to be alive in Him. I pray that all who know me will know that Jesus is Lord of my life. It's in His name that I pray. Amen.}

Digging Deeper

- Find a modern translation and read **Romans 6:1-14**. List the ways that God might be speaking to you personally.
- How do you define "addiction?" Do you believe that you have a food addiction? Why or why not? If you are still overeating compulsively, how might this passage renew your mind so that you might stop the devil dead in his tracks?
- Do you know other Born Again Christians who now have victory over compulsive overeating? Have you ever humbled yourself and gone to them for prayers and help with your eating?

DAY 49

Whoever can be trusted with very little can also be trusted with much, and whoever is dishonest with very little will also be dishonest with much.
Luke 16:10

ABSTINENCE IS FOOD HONESTY

In the devotional OUR DAILY BREAD[2], I found this little poem

When others view our lives today,
Our honesty is on display;
Lord, help us point the way to You
By doing what is kind and true. —*Branon*

When I read these verses, they made me think about my presence in the rooms of recovery. I stay in the program in order to point all to my Lord and Savior, Jesus Christ. Needless to say, I would be a poor witness if I did not keep my abstinence clean and committed.

My twenty-four hour commitment to eat abstinently puts my integrity on the line. I do not take this lightly, so I do not dare go out into the day "unarmed." I begin my morning with a sincere prayer of thanksgiving for making it through yesterday of not destroying myself with the food. I then ask for the willingness and strength to stay abstinent throughout the present day. I prayerfully draw near to God through His word, and I rely on His protection. My abstinence is in His hands. I pray to bring honor to Him in all that I do.

{Dear Father, I pray to remember that the world trusts less of what I say and watches more of what I do. Please keep me abstinent for Jesus' sake. I pray never to bring dishonor to

His name through gluttony and cheating. When it comes to being abstinent, I pray to let my "no be no." I pray this in the name of Jesus. Amen.}

Digging Deeper

- Read **Luke 16:10**. Underline words and phrases that speak to your heart. Look up the definitions of key words. Write a paraphrase of this passage and make a plan to put God's message into this day.
- How clean is your abstinence? Do you see clean abstinence as a way to witness to the non-believer? Why or why not?
- Look up each of the following verses and summarize what they teach about honesty: **2 Corinthians 8:21; 1 Peter 2:12; Psalm 24:3,4; Proverbs 11:1; and Proverbs 12:22.**

DAY 50

I will lie down and sleep in peace, for you alone,
O LORD,
make me dwell in safety.
Psalm 4:8

UNSHAKEABLE PEACE

Throughout his lifetime, David faced many life-threatening situations—defending his sheep from a lion, facing the giant Goliath, fleeing from King Saul for his life, and living in exile because his own son sought to kill him. Regardless of how bad the circumstances, David understood where he stood with God. He had the knowing assurance that God would be responsive to his prayers.

In Psalm 4, David reminds me that a clean heart gives me the confidence to approach the Lord unashamedly. My heart is clean because Jesus paid the price for my sins on the cross. I have put my trust for salvation in Jesus alone, and this has made me a true child of God. Therefore, there will never be a prayer that I make that will be ignored by my heavenly Father.

Even when circumstances are not the greatest on the outside, I can have peace on the inside by keeping my focus on the Lord. This inner peace assures me that I have found favor with God. When the day is done, I close my eyes and sleep in peace.

{Thank you, Father, for sending Jesus to save me. He has given me a joy, which is matchless! Thank you that I need not fear anything, for my soul has been "spoken for." In the name of Jesus, I give you thanks and praise. Amen.}

Digging Deeper

- Read **Psalm 4:7,8**. Underline words and phrases that speak to your heart. Look up the definitions of key words. Write a paraphrase of this passage and make a plan to put God's message into this day.
- What do you do when you cannot sleep? Someone once said that wakefulness in the night might be God calling. Have you ever tried reading the Bible and praying when you could not sleep?
- In the books of **1Samuel** and **2 Samuel** we learn much about David, "a man after God's own heart." Prayerfully consider reading these two books to learn more about this great king.

DAY 51

So he went down and dipped himself in the Jordan seven times, as the man of God had told him, and his flesh was restored and became clean like that of a young boy.
2 Kings 5:14

BECOMING TEACHABLE

Humbly following simple instructions can often mean the difference between relief and continued suffering. In 2 Kings 5:1-14, this lesson was learned by a successful commander. The commander's name was Naaman, and he was a highly admired officer of the army of Aram. However, Naaman suffered from leprosy.

One day, Naaman goes to the prophet Elisha's home because he has heard about the prophet's ability to heal. Upon arrival, one of Elisha's servants meets Naaman at the door with a message from Elisha. Naaman is told that if he wants to be healed, he must dip himself seven times in the Jordan River.

When Naaman hears these simple instructions, he becomes outrageously indignant. He turns to storm away, but his servants begin reasoning with him and convince him "not to give up before the miracle." Naaman swallows his pride and does what he is told. He dips himself seven times and is healed of his leprosy.

I identify so much with Naaman. One of the first things I heard in the program was that weighing and measuring my food without exception would stop the misery of overeating and help to bring much order into my life. I wanted those things, but the people-pleaser in me initially feared what "normal" people might think if I were to take out my cup, scale, and tablespoon. By the grace of God, though, I followed the directions of my sponsor and those who had gone before me. Many years later, I know the joy and freedom of continuous abstinence from compulsive overeating.

"Without exception, no matter what"—this act of humility gave me a starting point to becoming teachable in many other areas than just the food alone. I am learning that God is calling me to be a gentle and quiet student. I pray to cooperate with the Spirit's leading and to let Him teach me through His word.

{Dear Father, many times I am still like Naaman in that I cannot believe that your simple answers will bring the relief that I am seeking. I pray to let you speak to me through your word. I pray for the willingness to do what you tell me. In Jesus' name I pray. Amen.}

Digging Deeper

- Read the story about Naaman's healing in **2 Kings 5:1-14**. What are your favorite parts? Why?
- How clean is your abstinence? Are there still areas regarding your food where you are not following directions? Are you praying for the willingness to be willing?
- Some define humility as "teachability." Summarize what is learned in these verses about humility: **Proverbs 11:2**; **Philippians 2:5-8**; **Colossians 3:12**; and **1 Peter 5:5**.

DAY 52

He came to that which was his own, but his own did not receive him. Yet to all who received him, to those who believed in his name, he gave the right to become children of God—children born not of natural descent, nor of human decision or a husband's will, but born of God.
John 1:11-13

CHILDREN OF GOD

There is a popular teaching today that everyone is a child of God. This is not what the Bible teaches. Everyone is a creation of God, but only those who receive Jesus, who believe in His name, are children of God.

God loves us all, but as children of God we are co-heirs with Jesus. As children of God, we have the privilege of knowing God as Father. We have the confidence that He hears and attends to every prayer that we make.

Jesus gave up His life so that I might have eternal life. What a tremendous gift! I desire to please God in all that I say, think, and do. I want my food to be clean for Jesus' sake. I pray to be through, forever, with compulsive overeating. I want my behavior to fitting for a child of the King.

{Dear Father, what a privilege it is to call you "Father." Thank you for Jesus. Thank you for my salvation. I pray to run to you, today, and not to the food. I pray in the name of Jesus. Amen.}

Digging Deeper

- Read **John 1:11-13**. Underline words and phrases that speak to your heart. Look up the definitions of key words. Write a paraphrase of this passage and make a plan to put God's message into this day.
- Just for today, can you say in all honesty that you are through with compulsive overeating? Why or why not?
- How do you define "children of God?" Look up these verses and summarize what they say: **Romans 8:14; Galatians 3:24-26; Philippians 2:14-16;** and **1 John 3:7-10**.

DAY 53

Jesus looked at him and loved him. "One thing you lack,"
he said. "Go, sell everything you have and give to the
poor, and you will have treasure in heaven.
Then come, follow me."
Mark 10:21

TOO MANY RICHES

There have been times in my life when I could see where I wanted to be, but I was unwilling to give up what I already had in order to get there. My "riches" were more important than my dreams. I lost out on opportunities to grow because of greed.

The Bible tells the story of a young man who was attracted to Jesus and His teachings. He came to Jesus and asked, "What must I do to inherit eternal life?" When Jesus pointed his attention to commandments of the Law, he was quick to declare, "All these I have kept since I was a boy."

Reading on in the story, it ends sadly. To inherit eternal life, the young man could not have any false gods. Jesus had to be his greatest treasure. The Bible says of the young man, "He went away sad, because he had great wealth."

{Thank you, Father, for the faith you have given me to embrace the gift of salvation. Thank you for opening my eyes when I was foolishly loving my personal "treasures" and losing my soul. Thank you, Jesus, for saving me. It's in Your name that I pray. Amen.}

Digging Deeper

- Read **Mark 10:17-22**. Rewrite this passage in your own words. What are some of the main themes of this reading? What lessons might you apply in your own life?
- Are there aspects about your abstinence that you "treasure" at the expense of true integrity with your food? Are you still justifying and making excuses for your overeating?
- The problem is not in having riches. The problem is in putting one's trust in riches. We are to put our trust in God alone. Look up **1 Timothy 6:17** in several different versions of the Bible. Write out the verse in the version that speaks directly to your heart.

DAY 54

Be very careful, then, how you live—
not as unwise but as wise, making the most of every
opportunity, because the days are evil.
Ephesians 5:15,16

A PERFECT DAY FOR LIVING

The devil is about postponing God's good. Since he is the "father of lies" he is about making what's bad seem good and what's good seem bad. I wasted a lot of time waiting for the "Monday" when I was going to start eating right. The "voices" told me that my world would be lifeless if I couldn't break my abstinence once and awhile. What a big lie this turned out to be!

The Bible teaches me truth. It explains that the days in which I am now living are evil days and I have been saved to bring light into this present darkness. To do this effectively, I need to understand what God desires. If I am getting over a food binge, I'm "hung over" like one recovering from being drunk. I miss opportunities to score victories for the Lord. My life is on hold. This is a shame because God saved me for living.

To live my life to the fullest, I must desire to be controlled by the Spirit and to allow Him to permeate every aspect of my life. Instead of delaying good works, I need to take advantage of every opportunity. I have no time to waste by chasing the food as the unsaved do. Every moment as a new creation in Christ is precious.

{Dear Father, I pray to keep my mind clear. I pray not to be "drunk" from overeating compulsively and ruining my life. I pray to have the Spirit control me. I give thanks and praise in the name of Jesus. Amen.}

Digging Deeper

- Read **Ephesians 5: 15-20.** Make up a list of "do's" and 'don'ts" based on what you read.
- Are you postponing knowing the joy of clean, back-to-back abstinence? Are you still justifying your overeating by downplaying its severity? Are you failing to admit how much your spiritual effectiveness is hampered by the way you relate to food?
- Consider what lessons can you glean from these verses about overeating: **Ezekiel 16:49; Philippians 3:19; 1 Corinthians 6:12; and Jude 1:12.**

DAY 55

For you are a people holy to the LORD your God.
The LORD your God has chosen you out of all the
peoples on the face of the earth to be his people,
his treasured possession.
Deuteronomy 7:6

BELONGING TO GOD

In the rooms of recovery they repeat a phrase: "attraction and not promotion." Members are encouraged to live out the program in such a way that people will want to know what it is they have that is making the difference. My clean, back-to-back abstinence has drawn more people to me than hanging a sign in my front yard. People have come to me for help because they have been convinced more by what they have seen than what I ever could say about abstinence.

The same is true about spreading the Good News of Jesus Christ. When I "show my flesh" through rudeness, complaining, self-pity, bitterness, etc, I turn people off and scares them away. Regardless of my eloquence in speaking the truth, it won't matter if my actions are no different than the unsaved in my midst.

I can never afford to forget my purpose. This is why Jesus tells me to "abide" in Him (John 15:4,5). When I fix my eyes on Jesus as go out into my day, He directs my living so that I witness for Him in wonderful ways. Through His power, I do those things that strengthen my soul, lead others out of darkness, and cause the lost to be drawn into His light.

{Thank you for choosing me, Lord. Thank you for the abundant mercy that You have showered upon me through salvation. Convict me of sinful desires that threaten my witness. I pray to have a gentle and quiet spirit. Make me like you, Jesus. It's in Your name that I pray. Amen.}

Digging Deeper

- Read **Deuteronomy 7:6**. Underline words and phrases that speak to your heart. Look up the definitions of key words. Write a paraphrase of this verse and make a plan to put God's message into this day.
- Have you ever written out the story of your recovery from compulsive overeating? Writing out "where you were, what happened, and where you are today" might give you a greater appreciation for your abstinence and a greater compassion for those who "still suffer."
- As Christians, we are a chosen people, belonging to God. Read and summarize what the Bible says about this in these verses: **1 Peter 2:9-12; Romans 8:28-30; and Psalm 106:4,5.**

DAY 56

He who conceals his sins does not prosper,
but whoever confesses and renounces them finds mercy.
Proverbs 28:13

COMING CLEAN

From time to time, I have food dreams where I break my abstinence. Without fail, in the dream, I try to cover up my slip. Without fail, in the dream, I feel awful lying to my sponsor and my other friends in the program. I am always relieved when I wake up and find that I'm still abstinent.

If I want to feel the refreshment from the Lord again, I need to make up my mind to be done with my sin. When I conceal my sins, I'm still cherishing them in a way. That close feeling of sweet fellowship with the Lord still eludes me. The Bible teaches that I need to have sincere regret for my sins, to turn away from them and run back to God. This is the essence of repentance.

What a wonderful God I have; He wants me to feel His closeness. When sin has caused a break in this fellowship, He has provided a way out. It is found in **1 John 1:9**: *If we confess our sins, he is faithful and just and will forgive us our sins and purify us from all unrighteousness.*

{Dear Father, I pray to confess my sins and turn completely away from them. I want to feel your sure and promised forgiveness. Convict me of unconfessed sin. Restore my feelings of closeness to Jesus. I pray this in His holy name. Amen.}

Digging Deeper

- Read **Proverbs 28:13**. Underline words and phrases that speak to your heart. Look up the definitions of key words. Write a paraphrase of this verse and make a plan to put God's message into this day.
- Have you ever broken your abstinence? How did you handle letting your sponsor and friends know? What did you learn about "coming clean?"
- Our flesh tells us to deny and make excuses for our sins. God tells us to confess our sins. Summarize what you learn about confession from these verses: **Psalm 32:3-7; James 5:16; and Acts 3:19.**

DAY 57

Therefore, my dear brothers, stand firm.
Let nothing move you.
Always give yourselves fully to the work of the Lord,
because you know that your labor in the Lord
is not in vain.
1 Corinthians 15:58

STANDING FIRM

With great disdain, someone once said to me, "You are a good starter, but a poor finisher." Although I despised being criticized, I could not deny the truth in what they were saying.

My "lose-gain-lose-gain" dieting pattern was no secret to anyone. Equally easy to see was that I changed jobs every two to three years. My house contained more than its share of barely used materials and equipment for hobbies and projects that were gathering dust in storage.

In all honesty, I was a person who got discouraged easily and who frequently lost heart. The Bible says this: *Let us not become weary in doing good, for at the proper time we will reap a harvest if we do not give up* (**Galatians 6:9**). God calls me to "not give up before the miracle" because there will be a bountiful harvest, if I see things through to the end.

{Dear Father, strengthen me to deal with discouragement. Please help me to stay strong in the Lord and to not lose heart. Encourage me through your word. I pray to be an encouragement to others. I pray this in the name of Jesus. Amen.}

Digging Deeper

- Read **1 Corinthians 15:58**. Underline words and phrases that speak to your heart. Look up the definitions of key words. Write a paraphrase of this verse and make a plan to put God's message into this day.
- How would you describe the Lord's work through you in the twelve-step rooms? Describe a time when you felt discouraged? How did the Lord help you through this?
- If God encourages us, then we, His servants, must do the same. Read and summarize the following verses: **1 Thessalonians 3:2-4; Romans 1:11-12;** and **2 Timothy 4:2**.

DAY 58

Everyone must submit himself to the governing authorities, for there is no authority except that which God has established. The authorities that exist have been established by God.
Romans 13:1

SUBMITTING WITH JOY

It was hard for me to face the fact that if I wanted to mature, I needed to learn how to submit with joy. I have learned to thank God for my sponsor. With God's help, I am able to let go of what she cannot give me and embrace what she can.

The greatest gift that she gives me is her example of strong abstinence. She is committed to "not eat, no matter what". She works for her abstinence. She works to help me to stay abstinent. She is not my enemy but someone given to help me to be true to myself with the food. She leads by example and for this I am truly grateful.

Because I am God's child under the blood of Jesus, there is no relationship of mine about which He doesn't know or doesn't care. I can pray, and He will give me the willingness and strength to keep a positive and cooperative attitude regarding my sponsor at all times. In Him, sponsorship can always be a win-win situation.

{Thank you for my sponsor and her commitment to food honesty. Give me the willingness and the strength to learn from her abstinent example. I pray this in the name of Jesus. Amen.}

Digging Deeper

- Read **Romans 13:1-7**. Rewrite this passage in your own words. What are some of the main themes of this reading? What lessons might you apply in your own life?
- Which of your sponsees are a joy to sponsor? Why do you think this is so? How might your sponsor describe how it is to sponsor you? Are there changes you need to make in your attitude regarding submission?
- Have you been thinking (again?) about changing sponsors because of persecution or conflict over your Christian faith? Read this quote: This is found in the LIFE APPLICATION BIBLE[3]: *"Submission is voluntarily cooperating with someone, first out of love and respect for God and then out of love and respect for that person. Submitting to nonbelievers is difficult, but it is a vital part of leading them to Jesus Christ. We are not called to submit to nonbelievers to the point that we compromise our relationship with God, but we must look for every opportunity to humbly serve in the power of God's Spirit."*
- Then read **1 Peter 2:18-25, John 15:20-22, 2 Timothy 3:12,13,** and **1 Peter 4:12-19.** Summarize what is being taught. Write about what you are feeling. Ask another Christian in the rooms to pray with you, and for you, regarding this.

DAY 59

Even youths grow tired and weary, and young men
stumble and fall; but those who hope in the LORD
will renew their strength. They will soar on wings like
eagles; they will run and not grow weary,
they will walk and not be faint.
Isaiah 40:30,31

WAITING ON THE LORD

Praying the prayer, "Dear Lord, please keep me abstinent," helps me to patiently wait through the urge to overeat.
I am learning that overeating is often triggered by situations
that seem threatening and out of control. I am also learning
that circumstances change if I give them enough time. Instead
of thinking about food, I pray for strength. I then get busy on
godly activities until the situation changes.

In **Jeremiah 29:11,** this is written: *"For I know the plans*
I have for you," declares the LORD, "plans to prosper you
and not to harm you, plans to give you hope and a future."
Because it is "God's plan" for my life and not "my plan"
for my life, my impatience has the potential of delaying the
good that God has in store for me.

God has begun this good work in me, and He is in the
process of bringing it to completion (**Philippians 1:6**). He is
in control now. I pray to "get with the program" and let Him
have His way with me. It's not about me any more; it's all
about Him.

{Dear Father, please help me to remember that I am no
longer "running the show." Help me to grow in patience
and trust. Thank you for the next miracle that is soon to be
revealed in my life. I pray and give thanks in the name of
Jesus. Amen.}

Digging Deeper

- Read **Isaiah 40:30,31**. Underline words and phrases that speak to your heart. Look up the definitions of key words. Write a paraphrase of these verses and make a plan to put God's message into this day.
- What do you do when the urge to overeat pounces upon you? Have you shared this tip with someone who might be struggling with the food today? Are you willing to make an encouraging outreach call with God's help today?
- Use your concordance to find several verses about patience. Pray for the willingness to choose one to write down and commit to memory.

DAY 60

The eyes of the LORD are everywhere,
keeping watch on the wicked and the good.
Proverbs 15:3

MY OWN PLATE

God has given me my portion and my cup. I have a daily provision of food to eat, water to drink, and clothes to wear. God knows what I require, so I don't need to worry. But there have been times when I have looked over into my neighbor's "pasture" and have longed for what they've had. In comparison, what I had did not seem like enough. The Bible points out the foolishness of this endeavor and warns me against doing this.

The Twelve-Step programs have a similar warning. The slogan, "Keep your eyes on your own plate," is a reminder to take care of my own abstinence and to stop looking for an "easier, softer way" with the food. I have a sponsor who interprets and directs how I am to follow my food plan. She is sponsored using the same "bottom line" guidelines—honesty, rigor, and cleanness with the food. Food traditions that have worked over the years are wisely upheld.

I trust that others want recovery from compulsive over-eating as much as I do. Why activate my obsession and even bitterness by comparing what I do with what my neighbor does? If there is dishonesty, God will uncover it.

{Dear Father, please help me to sidestep the temptation to envy what others do with their food. I pray to embrace the abstinence that You have given to me and to follow my food guidelines honestly. I pray to eat in a way that honors You—each and every day. I pray this in the name of Jesus. Amen.}

Digging Deeper

- Read **Proverbs 15:3.** What does this verse mean, exactly? Write all that comes to your mind.
- Write about a time when you have envied what another was allowed to eat. What was the result of your jealousy?
- Read **Psalm 73.** How might this Psalm be seen in light of keeping your eyes on your own plate?

DAY 61

The LORD who delivered me from the paw of the lion and the paw of the bear will deliver me from the hand of this Philistine." Saul said to David, "Go, and the LORD be with you."
1 Samuel 17:37

FACING MY GOLIATH

1 Samuel 17 contains the story of David and Goliath: The Israelites were in a face-off with the Philistines. The Philistines held the advantage because of the nine-foot giant, Goliath of Gath, who was very insolent and sure of himself. For forty days, he taunted and terrified the Israelites by challenging them to send one of their men to fight against him and thus bring a quick end to the war.

David, a young shepherd boy, had been sent to the battlefield by his dad to bring provisions to his brothers. When David heard the defiant dare of Goliath, he was angered. David began asking around the camp about the situation and called for "this disgrace" to be removed. When King Saul found out, he sent for David. Standing before the king, David offered to go before Goliath and fight him.

Because of David's age, Saul initially tried to dissuade him. But David argued his case, citing times when he had faced foes and challenges and had been victorious by the grace of God. So, Saul let him face Goliath.

With a sling shot, a few stones, and a tremendous faith, David slew Goliath. Where men many years older and with more experience had failed to end this crisis, David was able because the battle was the Lord's. David trusted in God to "do for him what he couldn't do for himself." I pray that I do the same as I face my Goliath each and every day.

{Dear Father, every day there are things which threaten to terrify me and stop me in my tracks. I could easily forget that Jesus is my light and my salvation. Fill me with the Holy Spirit so that I can stand firm in the face of daily adversity. I pray in Jesus' name. Amen.}

Digging Deeper

- Read the story of David in Goliath in **1 Samuel 17:1-50**. What are your favorite parts? What, would you say, are key verses and why?
- Is compulsive overeating still a Goliath in your life? If you are abstinent, are there other food issues that defy you (i.e. weight gain, obsession with certain foods, envy of another's food plan, etc.)?
- Read these verses about God fighting for us. Chose a favorite: **1 Samuel 17:47; Psalm 144:1, 2 Chronicles 20:17;** and **Numbers 10:9**.

DAY 62

For nothing is impossible with God.
Luke 1:37

NO IMPOSSIBILITIES

I remember the desperation that I felt just before my last attempt to stop compulsive overeating. I had tried and failed so many times before. My head knew all the reasons why I should quit, but I just could not get my will to cooperate. It was only by God's grace and mercy that I made that one attempt more—to do the seemingly impossible.

God alone can do the impossible. As a Christian, I know that it does me no good to go around and chant: "I can do all things" or "All things work together for good," if I leave God out of the equation. Without Jesus I can do nothing. The Bible says that I can do all things *through Christ, who strengthens me* (**Philippians 4:13**). When things don't seem to be working out, the Bible reminds me that, all things work together for good *to those who love God, to those who all the called according to His purpose* (**Romans 8:28**).

Jesus did it all! His purity exposed my sinfulness. His death bridged the chasm between me and God the Father. Through His resurrection, I have hope that I can overcome all that is godless in my life. Jesus is my Lord and Savior, and in Him, there are no impossibilities.

{Dear Father, thank you for loving me so much that You sent Jesus to save me. I pray not to let Satan stop me in my tracks by his lies. I want to shine for Jesus. He has done so much for me. It's in His name that I pray. Amen.}

Digging Deeper

- Read **Luke 1:26-38**. What was the impossible situation facing Mary at the time? How might this passage be applicable in a situation that you are facing today?
- Are you still struggling to get abstinent? What spiritual things have you done today to cooperate with God regarding your abstinence? If you are abstinent, how have your reached out to encourage another who is struggling?
- God can do anything. Look up these verses and prayerfully consider making one a memory verse: **Luke 18:27; Mark 14:36; and Job 42:2.**

DAY 63

They did not destroy the peoples as the LORD had commanded them, but they mingled with the nations and adopted their customs.
Psalm 106:34,35

POISONOUS THINKING

It would always amaze me, on the other side of a binge that I could have been "so stupid" and hurt myself with the food again. It baffled me that I didn't stop my hand from reaching out for the extra food before it was too late. It took quite some years in recovery to truly understand that long before the binge began, my mind had gone to unsafe places with the food.

Someone has said that a food thought is a lot like a poisonous snake entering your house. Who would think to reach down, pick up the snake with their hands, and examine and cuddle it. Yet with food thoughts, I would do that very thing. Instead of praying for God to remove them, I would ponder the possibility and end up in another binge. I thank God that this is not the case today.

In my Christian life, I am learning that it is not just a food thought that has the possibility to destroy. There are other ungodly thoughts that flit into my head and are just as deadly. These thoughts should be annihilated immediately using prayer and the word of God! Failing to do so, put me at risk of going far, far off of God's path for my day. The promised pleasure is short-lived compared to the beating that the evil does to me.

{Dear Father, I pray to stay alert, knowing that the devil is always looking for new ways to destroy. Thank you for your Holy Spirit who trains my hands for battle. I have nothing

to fear. I pray to have the humility to let the Spirit lead me and teach me today. I pray to remember that love is a much better teacher than misery. I pray this in the name of Jesus. Amen.}

Digging Deeper

- **Psalms 105** and **106** give a mini-history of the Jewish people. Read these psalms, and write down the key highlights and patterns that you observe.
- Recall your last binge. Recall what was going on in your head (if you can) before you actually took the first compulsive bite. How might you have avoided overeating compulsively at that time?
- Throughout the Bible, we are warned that our character can become corrupted through the wrong associations. Read what these verses say and summarize the warning: **1 Corinthians 15:33; Proverbs 6:27-29; 2 Corinthians 6:14;** and **Hosea 9:10**.

DAY 64

Be joyful always; pray continually;
give thanks in all circumstances,
for this is God's will for you in Christ Jesus.
1 Thessalonians 5:16-18

BE JOYFUL ALWAYS

There is a world of difference between happiness and joy. Happiness is circumstantial. It's conditional on what is happening on the outside. If things are going the way that I think they should, then I am happy. Joy, on the other hand, is the inherent Christian quality of deep peace and inner gladness that rises up from the soul—even in the hard times.

Because Jesus is my Lord and Savior, I have the Holy Spirit living in me. When I ponder the value of this magnificent gift, I am filled with unspeakable joy! This Spirit was promised and has been delivered. He is my guarantee that at the end of this life as I know it, there will be so much good coming to me that my mind cannot even begin to wrap itself around the concept. I belong to the Father; He purchased me, and I have reason to shout, "Hallelujah!" (**Ephesians 1:13-14**).

My joy is based on the deep, deep love that God has for me. And this can never be taken away. *For I am convinced that neither death nor life, neither angels nor demons, neither the present nor the future, nor any powers, neither height nor depth, nor anything else in all creation, will be able to separate us from the love of God that is in Christ Jesus our Lord* (**Romans 8:38,39**).

{Dear Father, thank you for my salvation. Teach me daily how to live my life in joy. I pray to keep a grateful attitude in good times and in bad. It's in Jesus' name that I pray. Amen.}

Digging Deeper

- Read **1 Thessalonians 5:16-18**. Underline words and phrases that speak to your heart. Look up the definitions of key words. Write a paraphrase of this passage and make a plan to put God's message into this day.
- Write about an unhappy time when you were surprised by the joy that the Lord provided in the midst of your circumstances.
- Read these verses concerning joy. Summarize what they say: **John 16 22-24; Romans 5:9-11; 1 Peter 1:6-9; and Jude 1:24,25.**

DAY 65

What is more, I consider everything a loss compared to the surpassing greatness of knowing Christ Jesus my Lord, for whose sake I have lost all things. I consider them rubbish, that I may gain Christ and be found in him, not having a righteousness of my own that comes from the law, but that which is through faith in Christ—the righteousness that comes from God and is by faith.
Philippians 3:8,9

THE MOST IMPORTANT THING

At the time that it happened, reaching my goal weight through abstinence was an unbelievable accomplishment. It was nothing short of miracle. In order to get abstinent and stay abstinent, I had to be willing to talk with God. The result was that I began to trust prayer.

Praying gave me the feeling that I was spiritual. I found myself drawn to other "believers", and from time to time, I would come across people who had a deep and unshakeable faith. These people had a peace and poise about them that I found so attractive. They studied the Bible and lived it out in their lives. When they prayed, they prayed with power. They believed that they had a personal relationship with God, and I could see that they were not mistaken. I wanted what they had.

From them, I learned that God was a holy God and that even the smallest sin was a big problem to Him. I began to understand that even if I could write and give away a lifetime of inventories, it could never cover every transgression that I was capable of committing. I understood the need for a Savior, and in time, I cried out to Jesus to save me.

Jesus is my Lord and Savior. Knowing Him is the most important thing in my life today without exception. Without Him, I'm nothing. Because of Him, I have peace with God.

{Dear Father, thank you for loving the world so much that You gave your Son for our salvation. Thank You for eternal life. It's in Jesus' name that I pray. Amen.}

Digging Deeper

- Using a modern translation, read **Philippians 3:8,9.** What does this passage mean to you personally? Look up key words if it helps you to answer the question better.
- Write about your own "Adventures in Prayer." How and why did you begin to pray with all your heart?
- Read **John 3:3**. How do you define being "Born Again?" Do you consider yourself a Born Again Christian? Why or why not?

DAY 66

*After Jesus had gone indoors, his disciples asked him
privately, "Why couldn't we drive it out?" He replied,
"This kind can come out only by prayer."*
Mark 9:28, 29

DRIVING OUT STRONGHOLDS

Spiritual strongholds are sinful patterns of thinking and acting that have become so habitual that they block the light of truth. Those who have strongholds are often blinded to the sin that has become rampant within them. They justify their behavior through argument. They don't admit the sin and dismiss the seriousness of its presence.

Much has been spoken and written about the spiritual stronghold of racism in the church today. It has been said that more segregation occurs between the hours of 9 and 12 on a given Sunday morning than during any other time of the week. This saddens me.

The stronghold of overeating that I see running rampant in the church also saddens me. Some of the most beautifully, gifted children of God are being stopped in their tracks because they feel so ashamed about their body size. They are reluctant to be a "light on the hill" for fear that it might bring attention to their weight. Some, in the other extreme, pretend their weight doesn't matter to them, when it is so obvious to everyone else that it does.

I have prayed that the Lord would use me to help break these strongholds that I see in the church. For this to happen, the strongholds in my own life must be "named, claimed, and dumped." I pray that I will consistently ask God to convict me of the sin in my own life so that I might be used by Him to make a difference.

{Dear Father, open my eyes to the strongholds in my life. Let me not down play their seriousness. Keep me persistent in my prayers against my own strongholds and those of my brothers and sisters in Christ. I give thanks for the victory to come. In Jesus' name, I pray. Amen.}

Digging Deeper

- Study **2 Corinthians 10:3-6**. Write down anything you learned about tearing down spiritual strongholds.
- Are aspects of overeating still a stronghold in your life? What are you doing about this?
- Use a concordance to look up at least four verses on praying? How does your prayer life compare to what the word of God teaches?

DAY 67

How can a young man keep his way pure?
By living according to your word.
Psalm 119:9

KEEPING MY WAY PURE

One of the first things I learned in abstinence was the importance of reading the labels. Since there were definite substances that I avoided as part of my abstinence, I was taught to make sure that these things were not hidden within the ingredients of foods that might otherwise be allowable.

In my Christian walk, I have to watch out for things that might lead me down a sinful path. Many times these "contaminates" are hidden in activities and pastimes that seem harmless and innocent. If it were not for the Word of God I might be easily led astray.

The Bible has become my standard. If something goes against the Word of God, regardless of how cute and sweet it appears, I have learned to see it as sin—which has the power to destroy. God has given me the scripture to see sin behind its clever disguises. What a good and loving God I have!

{Dear Father, teach me what the Bible says and strengthen me to be obedient. Thank you for the wisdom I learn through living out the commands that you give in your word. In the name of Jesus, I pray. Amen.}

Digging Deeper

- Read **Psalm 119: 9-16**. Look closely at the verbs in this passage. Write down the things that God is teaching you in this passage?
- How diligent are you in reading labels? Do you ask the waiter about the contents of the foods on the menu? Why is this important?
- We must be smart and watch out for the devil's traps. Read and summarize what these two Bible verses teach about vigilance: **1 Peter 5:8** and **Ephesians 6:17,18**.

DAY 68

Therefore, prepare your minds for action;
be self-controlled; set your hope fully on the grace
to be given you when Jesus Christ is revealed. As obedient
children, do not conform to the evil desires you had when
you lived in ignorance. But just as he who called you is
holy, so be holy in all you do; for it is written:
"Be holy, because I am holy."
1 Peter 1:13-16

HOLINESS

To be holy is to be set apart for the glory of God. I was saved from a life of destruction, and God calls me to be holy. This is not always easy in a world where holiness is misunderstood and disregarded. I must look to the Bible to find instructions on how this is lived out.

In **Psalm 119:9-16**, the Spirit speaks to my heart. Here are some questions I might ask myself in the process of doing a "spot-check inventory":

- How have I lived out the Word of God in my life today?
- Have I asked the Lord to show me if and how I have strayed from what He desires in my life today?
- How much time today did I give to Bible memory?
- What did the Lord show me in His Word today? Did I thank Him?
- Who have I spoken with today about the Word of the Lord?
- Did I have time apart with the Lord to pray, read His Word, and reflect upon it?
- Did I make the time to rejoice in the Lord?

As I focus on the things of God, the things of my former life lose their appeal. As I focus on Jesus, all that I knew before knowing Him is like rubbish. I want to be holy because Jesus is holy, and I want to be like Him.

{Dear Father, thank you for my salvation. I want to grow in my faith. Please teach me through your word how to be holy and strong. I pray this in the name of Jesus. Amen.}

Digging Deeper

- Read **1 Peter 1:13-16**. Underline words and phrases that speak to your heart. Look up the definitions of key words. Write a paraphrase of this passage and make a plan to put God's word into action.
- How does abstinence fit into God's plan of holiness for your life?
- Study **Colossians 3: 1-17**. Write some questions you might use to evaluate your progress in growing in holiness.

DAY 69

If your right eye causes you to sin, gouge it out and throw it away. It is better for you to lose one part of your body than for your whole body to be thrown into hell. And if your right hand causes you to sin, cut it off and throw it away. It is better for you to lose one part of your body than for your whole body to go into hell.
Matthew 5:29,30

UNSHACKLED

Because my overeating was often done in secret, many people have no idea how much food I could eat on a binge. Sometimes, I even shocked myself. I would be home alone. I would remember opening the huge bag of carbohydrate, and before very long, I would be eating the last one. I somehow would blank out the many trips I had to make to the kitchen to get more and more. Eventually, though, I had to face the reality that I had eaten "the whole thing"—again!

Weighing and measuring without exception, no matter what, is how I "gouge out" and "cut off" that which caused me to sin (**Matthew 5:29,30**). I have been redeemed, and I desire to run the good race for Jesus' sake.

So, when well meaning people ask, "Do you have to weigh your food *this* time? Can't you just 'eyeball' it?" I have learned not to get angry or take their questions to heart. I see a bigger picture. It is not about a "diet" anymore; it is about being a winner in a spiritual battle.

"Therefore, since we are surrounded by such a great cloud of witnesses, let us throw off everything that hinders and the sin that so easily entangles, and let us run with perseverance the race marked out for us." ~ Hebrews 12:1

{Thank you for opening my eyes. Overeating was hindering me and placing me in shackles. Thank you for my abstinence. I pray for the willingness to be clean and disciplined with my food—each and every day. I pray in the name of Jesus. Amen.}

Digging Deeper

- Read **Matthew 5:29,30**. Underline words and phrases that speak to your heart. Look up the definitions of key words. Write a paraphrase of this passage and make a plan to put God's word into action.
- What is your history with overeating? How has it hindered and enslaved you? Do you see overeating as sinful for you? Why or why not?
- What message is God giving you in **Philippians 3:18-20**?

DAY 70

*Therefore, I urge you, brothers, in view of God's mercy,
to offer your bodies as living sacrifices, holy and pleasing
to God—this is your spiritual act of worship.*
Romans 12:1

A LIVING SACRIFICE

As I looked around at people who have many years of abstinence, I see that they are in the habit of "giving away what was given to them." In other words, they are out there carrying the message. They lead meetings; they sponsor people; they make and take outreach calls—whatever the need, they will do what they can to help carry the load.

As a Christian, I have been called to carry the message of salvation in everything that I do. I have not been saved to have a "wet rag" of a life. I have not been saved to go through life like a cloud with no direction. As Rick Warren would say, I have been called to have a "purpose-driven" life, and this purpose is to know Jesus and to make Him known.

I am abstinent today because of the mercy of God. He has provided a skillful way of eating that controls both the obsession with food and the compulsion to overeat. I pray to stay abstinent each and every day so that I can bring tribute to Him through my life. Because there are so many "in the rooms" who are seeking to know God, I want to be a godly example of one who has found Him. What He has done for me is priceless. To offer myself to Him is an honor.

{Dear Father, take my eyes, my mouth, my arms, my legs—take every part of me. I want to be an instrument of your righteousness. I pray that I live my life with an attitude of thanksgiving for all that Jesus has done. It's in His name that I pray. Amen.}

Digging Deeper

- Read **Romans 12:1**. Underline words and phrases that speak to your heart. Look up the definitions of key words. Write a paraphrase of this passage and make a plan to put God's word into action.
- Do you give God the credit for defining your abstinence and keeping you clean? Why or why not?
- One of the supreme acts of sacrifice is to "love the un-loveable." Read **1 Corinthians 13:1-7** and pray. Write out three possible demonstrations of love that you can show toward those in your life who are hard to love.

DAY 71

Love is patient, love is kind. It does not envy, it does not boast, its not proud. It's not rude, it is not self-seeking, it is not easily angered, it keeps no record of wrongs. Love does not delight in evil, but rejoices with the truth. It always protects, always trusts, always hopes, always perseveres. Love never fails.
1 Corinthians 13:4-8

PRAYING TO BECOME MORE LOVING

When I was a new Christian, I worked to memorize the passage found in **1 Corinthians 13:4-8** because it gave me a sensible way to practice love. Recently, my daily Bible reading brought me back to these verses. This is how the Spirit enlarged on this teaching by showing me ways to pray:

- I pray not to run ahead of the Spirit, but to wait for the Lord. He will reveal His perfect time and plan for action. I pray to follow His lead.
- I pray to show compassion and kindness to those the Lord brings into my day.
- I pray to enjoy the things that God has already given to me. I pray to stop lusting after that which is not mine.
- I pray to give God the glory. He has given me every good thing in my life, I cannot take credit for any of it.
- I pray to bring the Lord into every decision that at make and every task that I do.
- I pray to share God's revelation with gentleness and respect.
- I pray to have godly motives behind all that I do. It's not "my will" but "Thy will" be done.

- I pray to remember that behind most anger is fear. I pray to let faith not fear reign in my life.
- I pray that the Lord will show me my hidden bitterness. I pray that He will rout it out with perfect love and forgiveness.
- I pray not to let my eyes, ears, and mind be drawn to the sensationalizing of man's brokenness. I pray that the Lord will give me the willingness, strength, and creativity to lend a hand toward the solution today.
- I pray to learn more and more how to find my highest delight in God.
- I pray to make the time to train the hands of others against evil—just as the Lord has trained me.
- I pray to side-step the Devil's D's[4]: doubt, diversion, discouragement, despair, and delay.
- I pray to remember that the war has already been won for me. Jesus IS coming back and He WILL take me home. I pray to count on His renewing strength so that I can carry on the work of the Kingdom until He returns.
- I pray to remember that in Jesus, I cannot fail. I know Him. I have been called according to His purpose. He will work it out! (**Romans 8:28**)

{Father, I thank You. You never fail to stop teaching me. Thank you for the Bible and the truth it contains that is fresh and renewing each day. I pray and give thanks in the name of Jesus. Amen.}

Digging Deeper

- What is one of your favorite Bible verses? Ask the Spirit to help you to read and study it today with fresh, new eyes. Write down your revelation.
- How does abstinence helps you to be a more loving person?

The apostle John has written much about love in **1 John 4: 7-21**. Read this passage and write about how God is speaking to you through His word.

DAY 72

*Yet at the same time many even among the leaders
believed in him. But because of the Pharisees they would
not confess their faith for fear they would be put out of
the synagogue; for they loved praise from men
more than praise from God.*
John 12:42,43

GOD'S APPROVAL AND PRAISE

My history includes a time when what other people
thought of me was my main preoccupation. My life was
about impressing others. I somehow thought that if I could
gain the recognition, approval, and praise of those around
me, then I would "have it made."

When I think back, this is such a foolish endeavor. It
assumes that I can get into the mind of a person and know
what they are thinking. It also assumes that I am so important that I am the main attraction in the lives of others. Living
for the approval of others brings only anxiety, duplicity, and
frustration into my life.

As a Christian, what God thinks about me should be my
standard. He is my boss. He directs all that I think and all
that I do. However, this does not mean that I am insensitive
to what others say and think about me. Since God desires
that I work among people and draw them to Him, their feedback is important. Yet, it cannot be the driving force of what
I choose to do for the glory of God. Never again am I to fear
how others might judge. My goal is to please God, and it's
His praise I seek and not that of mankind.

{Dear Father, please give me the wisdom, courage and strength to witness well for Jesus. Please convict me when my fears are holding me back. I pray to make your approval my goal. I pray this in the name of Jesus. Amen.}

Digging Deeper

- Read **John 12:37-50**. Summarize what is happening in this passage. What lessons of living do you learn? How might you apply these into your own life?
- How would you define "people pleasing?" What has been your experience regarding people pleasing? Some people believe that overeating and people pleasing go hand-in-hand. Do you agree? Why or why not?
- Victory in living for God requires the Holy Spirit. Read **Acts 5:29-32**. Summarize what is happening in this passage. What lessons of living do you learn? How might you apply these into your own life?

DAY 73

*Be kind and compassionate to one another,
forgiving each other,
just as in Christ God forgave you.*
Ephesians 4:32

FORGIVENESS

When my life is on the upswing, it's easy to have a forgiving heart. But when my feelings have been hurt and my plans are not working out, my flesh looks for a person to criticize and to be the object of my bitterness. Many times, I can know in my head that I must drop the anger and disappointment, but my flesh refuses to cooperate. What I need is a mind renewal so that I might experience a transformation (**Romans 12:2**).

I have found these four thoughts to be helpful to bring to mind when my bitterness is standing in the way of forgiving my neighbor:

1) **It's not about me; it's about Jesus.** Paul said that he had been crucified with Christ (**Galatians 2:20**). My bitterness is tied into a disappointment, which usually points back to the fact that I have tried to get back into the "driver's seat."

2) **My feelings of bitterness can usually be traced back to a lie that I have listened to and believed.** The word of God can be like a life preserver at a time like this. It can float me out of the muddy waters.

3) **Despite my filth and encrusted grit, Jesus showed compassion and pardoned my sin.** What gives me the right to hold something against another? Do I think that I am better than Jesus?

4) **When I cry aloud to Jesus, things change.** Dropping to my knees and admitting my powerlessness ushers

in the humility. When I am teachable, God can work to change me.

{Dear Father, thank you for giving me new life. Continue to expose my unforgiveness. I pray for a truly loving heart and the humility to cry out. Please transform my heart and change my thinking. I pray this in the name of Jesus. Amen.}

Digging Deeper

- Read **Ephesians 4:29-32**. Make a side-by-side list of dos and don'ts from this reading.
- Write about how your lack of forgiveness is tied in closely with you overeating. Give some concrete examples.
- Use a concordance and find several verses on forgiveness. Prayerfully ask for the willingness and strength to memorize a new verse today.

DAY 74

O God, you are my God, earnestly I seek you; my soul thirsts for you, my body longs for you, in a dry and weary land where there is no water.
Psalm 63:1

PURSUING JESUS

I would go to great lengths to have a delightful experience with the food. If someone told me that a certain restaurant was good, I made plans to get there. It didn't matter how far away it was or how much it cost. I schemed and planned; I maneuvered money and time. I did whatever it took to eventually taste for myself if the food there was all that others said it was.

The Bible says in **Psalm 34:8**, "Taste and see that the LORD is good." Just like I didn't take another's word for whether a restaurant was good enough, I am finding that I must experience God for myself to know truly of His goodness. I experience God for myself through Jesus.

True recovery happens as I learn to pursue Jesus with as much rigor as I had used in the pursuit of food. When I do, my soul finds pleasure beyond description.

{Dear Jesus, you are more precious than silver or gold. I pray to run hard after you. I pray to find my highest delight in your presence. I pray in Your holy name. Amen.}

Digging Deeper

- Read **Psalm 63:1**. Underline words and phrases that speak to your heart. Look up the definitions of key words. Write a paraphrase of this verse and make a plan to put God's word into action.
- How much time are you spending each day on the things of God? How does it honestly compare with the time that you are spending on food stuff? (Don't forget to count the mind time.) Are you willing to pray to pursue Jesus more?
- Read **Psalm 42:1-11** in several versions. Ask the Spirit to speak to your heart regarding this psalm. Write down what you are thinking and feeling.

DAY 75

We are hard pressed on every side, but not crushed;
perplexed, but not in despair; persecuted, but not
abandoned; struck down, but not destroyed.
We always carry around in our body the death of Jesus,
so that the life of Jesus may also be revealed in our body.
2 Corinthians 4:8-10

NOT IN DESPAIR

There was a time in my life when I never could say, "I don't know" and let it go at that. My pride was such that I always had to have an answer.

Because Jesus is my Lord, I have been given a built-in teacher—the Holy Spirit. The Spirit counsels me and instructs me (**John 14:26**). Even so, I still come face-to-face with perplexing mysteries of life that could drive me to despair, but I don't let them. I am learning to live with the unanswered questions in my life. I remember what one of my favorite Bible teachers would say, "Don't let what you DON'T know, stand in the way of what you DO know."

I DO know that I have been redeemed and that I have been given eternal life. I DO know that I belong to Jesus and He is coming back for me one day. There is no "unknown" on earth that can top these realities! With such assurance, despairing over the perplexing is not an option.

{Dear Father, I pray not to let the devil stop me in my tracks by pondering that which is not mine to know right now. I pray to place the unanswerable into the loving hands of Jesus and to leave it there. I pray this in His holy name. Amen.}

Digging Deeper

- In some Bibles, **2 Corinthians 4:1-18** has been titled "Treasures in Jars of Clay." Read this passage carefully and make notes of the important teachings that are given. Why do you think it was titled as such? How is the Spirit speaking to you regarding this?
- Are you (or someone you know) "into the food?" How might despairing over unanswerable questions be playing a part in your compulsive overeating? Are you willing to pray for the willingness to let Jesus be Lord of the unknowns in your life?
- When I have found it hard to let go of the unanswerable, I remember **Psalm 131:1,2**. Talk to the Lord about committing these verses to memory if questioning is sometimes a problem.

DAY 76

Answer me, O LORD, answer me, so these people will know that you, O LORD, are God, and that you are turning their hearts back again.
1 Kings 18:37

PRAYING WITH POWER

I can remember a time when I only knew how to pray "ready-made" prayers. These were said over and over again, alone or in unison with other churchgoers.

When I came into the rooms of recovery, I was encouraged to pray what was on my heart. From uninterrupted sharing, I had learned how to speak out my feelings. When I prayed my feelings, I felt like I was moving closer to God.

Every once in a while, though, I would come across people who spoke to God so honestly and confidently, that the power in their prayers "blew me away." Their prayers shook my heart and I knew God was listening. I wanted to learn how to pray like that. I thought it was a matter of skill. I was wrong.

Powerful praying is a matter of righteousness. Righteousness is a matter of Jesus. Because He is my Lord and Savior, I can approach God and call Him my Father. God listens to me because of who I am in Christ. I have confidence that my prayers will make a difference. This does not mean that God will always answer "Yes" to my prayers, but I know that even His "No" will prove to be a good thing.

{Dear Father, thank you for the righteousness of Jesus that is the power behind each prayer that reaches your heart. I pray to remember what length Jesus went to so that I might pray with such boldness and confidence. May I never take pride in this gift. May I always pray sincerely in the name of Jesus. Amen.}

Digging Deeper

- Read **James 5:16**. Underline words and phrases that speak to your heart. Look up the definitions of key words. Write a paraphrase of this verse and make a plan to put God's word into action.
- Are you abstinent, but still very restless? Do you know that you can have peace in Jesus? Are you Born Again? If you aren't sure, go to www.needhim. org or call 1-888-NEEDHIM.
- Some people are genuinely Born Again but they fear not praying "in the right way." I found a verse that gave me freedom to come to God in prayer about anything. Look up **Philippians 4:6** and consider hiding this verse in your heart.

DAY 77

All Scripture is God-breathed and is useful for teaching,
rebuking, correcting and training in righteousness, so
that the man of God may be thoroughly equipped for
every good work.
2 Timothy 3:16,17

GOD-BREATHED

I grew up in a tradition in which passages from the Bible were read at each service. Even so, I was not encouraged to study the whole Word of God. Whenever I happened upon passages that were harsh and senseless to my way of thinking, I tended to agree with those who taught that the Bible, on the whole, could not be taken literally. To them, to believe that the whole Bible was God-inspired was, at best, an "uneducated" way of thinking. At worse, it was down right dangerous. So my approach was like theirs: Take what you like and leave the rest.

Through Christian radio, I heard different teachers, who unashamedly stood firm in their belief that the entire Bible (from Genesis to Revelation) is the truth of God. They taught with authority, and I was drawn to what they shared. I learned why I was searching and how I could find what my heart was seeking. I needed to be saved. I needed to be directed. I needed Jesus. I need Jesus.

Taking the smorgasbord approach to the truth of the Bible is not what I do today. I want to love mankind in the way that Jesus did. The Bible has been given so that I might be equipped to go about this. I pray to take the whole Word, into the whole world, for Jesus' sake.

{Dear Father, thank you for the truth of the Bible. Thank you for men and women who teach without compromise, the whole Word of God. In the name of Jesus, I pray. Amen.}

Digging Deeper

- Read **2 Timothy 3:16, 17.** Underline words and phrases that speak to your heart. Look up the definitions of key words. Write a paraphrase of this passage and make a plan to put God's word into action.
- Are you abstinent, but still very restless? Do you know that you can have peace in Jesus? Are you Born Again? If you aren't sure, go to <u>www.needhim. org</u> or call 1-888-NEEDHIM.
- Read these verses concerning the Bible. Summarize what they say: **2 Timothy 2:15; James 1:22; Psalm 1:2,3;** and **Psalm 119:165.**

DAY 78

Praise be to you, O LORD; teach me your decrees.
With my lips I recount all the laws that come from
your mouth. I rejoice in following your statutes as one
rejoices in great riches. I meditate on your precepts and
consider your ways. I delight in your decrees;
I will not neglect your word.
Psalm 119:12-16

A PLEASANT ENDEAVOR

My first days of abstinence were not pleasant. It was difficult not feeling sad and depressed because my "goodies" had been "taken away." As time went on and my days of back-to-back abstinence grew, I came to enjoy my new way of eating. My taste buds learned to savor the flavor of the unrefined, natural state of foods. I would have never believed it!

Bible study was once seen as something unfamiliar and often hard to do. I certainly would not describe it then as pleasurable. My flesh was used to being in control, and it raged an all-out war against anything that threatened its dictatorship. Bible study was more of a "should do" rather than a "want to."

Today, it is different. Learning and applying the Word of God has become a pleasant endeavor. Through doing so, I can sense my growth; I can feel the loving hand of the Father. I am being trained and equipped by His every word, and this brings me joy.

{Dear Father, thank you for the power to change. You word is truly a lamp to my feet and a light to my path. I pray to always find delight in learning and applying your teaching. I pray in the name of Jesus. Amen.}

Digging Deeper

- Read **Psalm 119:12-16**. List some things that you might cultivate to hasten your growth toward delighting in the Word of God.
- Have you learned how to enjoy your abstinence without obsessing about food? How did it come about? What would you say to the newcomer who worries about this?
- Read **Psalm 1:1,2**. Paraphrase these verses. What additional things do you learn regarding how to delight in the Word of God?

DAY 79

*He wanted to see who Jesus was, but being a short man
he could not, because of the crowd. So he ran ahead
and climbed a sycamore-fig tree to see him,
since Jesus was coming that way.*
Luke 19:3-4

GOING TO ANY LENGTH

I was told that enthusiasm was very important in order
to stay abstinent. I was encouraged to cultivate a willingness
to go that extra mile for my abstinence. This meant bringing
"back-up," packing "hostage meals," asking about ingredients in restaurants, choosing other menu items when ingredients were questionable or unknown, etc., etc. Although it
was always hard *before* doing these things, I always felt like
a millionaire *after* I did them and preserved my abstinence—
despite how silly it appeared to others.

In **Luke 19**, there is the story of a businessman who
risked looking foolish in order to see Jesus. The man's name
was Zacchaeus. The Bible says that he was wealthy and also
short.

Jesus was passing through Jericho and Zacchaeus
wanted to see Him. The crowd was big and was in the way,
so Zacchaeus ran ahead and climbed up a tree in order to get
a glimpse of Jesus.

What a blessing Zacchaeus received! When Jesus
reached the spot where he perched, Jesus acknowledged
Zacchaeus and announced that He was coming to his house
that very day.

*{Dear Father, I pray to go to any length to persevere and
grow in my faith. I pray to risk looking like a fool for the
cause of Jesus. I pray in His name. Amen.}*

Digging Deeper

- Read the story of Zacchaeus in **Luke 19:1-10**. Retell the story in your own words. Have you gotten to the point in your own life that your faith is most important?
- Tell of a time when you went to any length to get abstinent food. Who encouraged (or discouraged) you? How did you feel later?
- Jesus knew who Zacchaeus was, and He called him by name. Read these verses and summarize what they say about the Lord knowing His own: **John 10:27; 2 Timothy 2:19; 1 Corinthians 8:3;** and **Jeremiah 1:5**.

DAY 80

He replied, "I tell you that to everyone who has,
more will be given, but as for the one who has nothing,
even what he has will be taken away."
Luke 19:26

VALUING THE VALUABLE

Once, I lost my abstinence. It was after I had about 4 ½ years. I can remember thinking, in the middle of the relapse, that I had been such a fool! I did not know what a valuable gift I had been given until I no longer had it.

I have learned in my Christian walk that when I was born again I was given a spiritual gift to be used to spread the Good News and to encourage the brethren. I am grateful for pastors who encouraged me to identify my gift and to find a place in the church and in the community where I could use it.

The more I use my gift, the more I value it. If I would just "sit on it," I would never experience how wonderful it feels to be used by God in powerful ways. My gift would soon become worth very little to me, and I would squander it. Eventually it would be as if I had lost the gift altogether, and someday, I would.

{Dear Father, I pray to be a good steward of the talents and gifts that you have given to me. Thank you for the experience of seeing them multiply through obedience. You are such an abundant giver. Thank you for loving me so much. In Jesus' name, I pray. Amen.}

Digging Deeper

- Read **Luke 19:26** in two or three different versions of the Bible. What is the meaning of this verse? If necessary, see what others have said in one or two different Bible commentaries.
- Do you value your abstinence? What things justify your answer to this question?
- If you have never identified your spiritual gift, a helpful tool for this can be found at www.teamministry.com. [5]

DAY 81

Some people have gotten out of the habit of meeting for worship, but we must not do that. We should keep on encouraging each other, especially since you know that the day of the Lord's coming is getting closer.
Hebrews 10:25

MY HOME AWAY FROM HOME

In my local church, I learn about God from the people of God. Week after week as we meet together for praise and worship, I grow in my love for them, and they for me. Until Jesus returns, my church is my home away from home where I learn and grow to be a better Christian.

Together we pray and watch God work miracles of change in our lives. Together we study the word and increase our understanding through our sharing. We encourage one another to walk in the love and light of Jesus. We are brothers and sisters in the Lord. We are an eternal family.

The devil would love for me to focus on the growing pains that we experience from time to time, but I won't do it! With God's help I can look above the imperfections of our flesh, knowing that one day we will be made perfect. With God's help we can love and forgive one another and work together for the kingdom—for Jesus' sake.

{Thank you for my local church. Thank you for love in action. As a congregation, please protect us from ourselves. Give us each a heart of forgiveness. Guide us to encourage one another in love. I pray in the name of Jesus. Amen.}

Digging Deeper

- Read **Hebrews 10:19-25**. Summarize what is being taught in this passage. What might God be saying to you personally? Write out a plan for putting God's word into action for this day.
- Where do you get group encouragement for your abstinence? How has this changed since when you were first abstinent? Why?
- Write down the history of your church participation. Note how you participated and contributed to the vitality of your church. If you are not in a church are you willing to pray that God will lead you to a Bible-teaching, Bible-believing church? If not, why not?

DAY 82

And the Lord's servant must not quarrel; instead,
he must be kind to everyone, able to teach, not resentful.
Those who oppose him he must gently instruct,
in the hope that God will grant them repentance leading
them to a knowledge of the truth, and that they will come
to their senses and escape from the trap of the devil,
who has taken them captive to do his will.
2 Timothy 2:24-26

THE PATIENT TEACHER

From time to time, I have run across students who are itching to argue. In **Luke 20**, Jesus encounters some in His audience, like these, who are contrary and oppose His teachings.

The chapter begins with Jesus' authority being questioned by the chief priest and the teachers of the Law (**20:1-8**). Later, some spies question Jesus about taxes in the hope of catching blasphemy in something that He would say (**20:20-26**). Then the Sadducees, who do not believe in resurrection, bring to Jesus a ridiculous "what if" situation about resurrection involving a widow and seven brothers (**20:27-40**).

Through it all, Jesus is divinely patient. He continues to teach with kindness, compassion and a deep desire to reach the heart of the lost. Jesus is the master teacher. I pray to be like Him.

{Dear Jesus, I pray not to quarrel with those who oppose me. I pray to teach without resentment. Fill me with your Spirit so that I might teach like You. It's in your name that I pray. Amen.}

Digging Deeper

- Read **Luke 20**. Note the sub-headings. Summarize their content.
- How do you respond when other oppose your abstinence? What lesson might you learn from **2 Timothy 2:24-26** in dealing with such opposition.
- Read **Philippians 2:14-16**. Define key words and paraphrase these verses. How might you apply what they teach in your life today?

DAY 83

For in the day of trouble he will keep me safe in his dwelling; he will hide me in the shelter of his tabernacle and set me high upon a rock.
Psalm 27:5

A PLACE OF SAFETY

When natural disasters strike, I am amazed at how quickly so much can be destroyed. The same is true in my thought life. There are days when the "voices of the evil one" attack with legions of warriors. Their threats are frightening, and I have come close to losing it all—fearing that depression and hopelessness will swallow me up.

Yet, I have been held in safety through the truth of God's word. Verses that I have hidden in my heart rise to the surface and remind me who I am in Christ Jesus. Again I hear the truth—I have been chosen; I belong to God. What force in this world is greater than the Spirit of Jesus who lives in my heart?

God's word is a place of safety. It is a secure dwelling place high above that which threatens to bring me down. Hallelujah! My God reigns!

{Dear Father, thank You for your word, the Bible. I pray to study it diligently and apply it faithfully. In Jesus' name, I pray. Amen.}

Digging Deeper

- (Add bullet about top verse)
- Have you found and memorized verses that encourage you to stay abstinent? Three to consider might be: **1 Corinthians 6:19,20; Matthew 5:29,30;** and **Philippians 3:18, 19**.
- Is Bible memory a vital spiritual discipline in your life? If not, will you pray right now for the willingness make it so?

DAY 84

Every good and perfect gift is from above, coming down from the Father of the heavenly lights, who does not change like shifting shadows.
James 1:17

GOOD GIFTS

The Sabbath was one of God's gifts to the Jewish people. It was not only a time to praise the LORD and enjoy Him, but it was also a time to rest from work in order to be refreshed and restored. Yet, for the Jewish leaders of Jesus' day, the Sabbath had become more important than God himself.

I must be careful not to fall victim to the same kind of behavior. I must give God first place in my life. I must worship the Giver and never the gift.

I am so grateful to be abstinent. I pray to never fail to tell others that I am abstinent today only by the grace of God. I pray to worship God and not my abstinence.

{Dear Father, you have blessed me richly. I pray to keep my focus fixed on the cross so that may never put a false god before You. I pray this in Jesus' name.}

Digging Deeper

- Read **James 1:17** from several different translations. Write your own paraphrase of this verse. Make plans to put this verse into action in this day.
- Tell how you became abstinent. Would you say that your abstinence is a gift from God?
- Read **Luke 6**, paying close attention to references about the Sabbath. What is your understanding of the Sabbath? Do you take a "Sabbath" each week?

DAY 85

*But love your enemies, do good to them, and lend to them
without expecting to get anything back. Then your reward
will be great, and you will be sons of the Most High,
because he is kind to the ungrateful and wicked.
Be merciful, just as your Father is merciful.*
Luke 6:35, 36

LOVING THE UNLOVABLE

God can change a life. I have seen this happen time and
time again. I have seen people who were once bitter, full
of rage, depressed, hopeless, unproductive, and sickened by
overeating be transformed into new creations. This is only
possible through the power of God.

God works through obedient people. As a Christian, I
have been commanded to go that "extra mile" with those
who affect me in adverse ways. In spite of their hatefulness toward me, I have been called to be loving, giving, and
merciful toward them.

Without the Holy Spirit, this would be utterly impossible.
The Holy Spirit provides the power to love supernaturally.
Because Jesus loves me, I am capable of loving in a way that
defies my flesh. To see this miracle in action is a reward unto
itself.

*{Father, I pray to remember that I am your child—called to
be set apart for kingdom work. Convict me when I am letting
the hardness of a challenge threaten to discourage me. Keep
me strong to persevere and to bring your love into the dark
and unloving situations that I presently face. I pray to feel
you near me. I pray in the name of Jesus. Amen.}*

Digging Deeper

- *The Bible Knowledge Commentary*[6] points out that there are seven aspects of unconditional love found in **Luke 6:27-38**. See how many of these seven you can discover for yourself .
- How does compulsive overeating, bitterness, and rage relate, in your own past history?
- List those who are challenges to you because of their hatefulness. Read **1 Corinthians 13:1-8.** Are you willing to pray to practice being loving toward them using these verses as goals?

DAY 86

Blessed are they whose ways are blameless,
who walk according to the law of the LORD.
Psalm 119:1

KEEPING BLAMELESS

There were times in my overeating career when I would have no idea how I started to binge again. I knew very little about how my feelings and moods were affected by my thoughts and attitudes. I didn't realize that harboring anger and resentment was a set up for compulsive overeating.

Others, who had gone before me, shared what they learned. In time, I could see the binge coming because I was equipped with knowledge about the nature of the beast.

As a Christian, the Bible has been given to equip me to side-step the pitfall of sinful behavior. There is a saying: "Either the Bible will keep you away from sin or sin will keep you away from the Bible." Each day I have a choice to make. Will I let myself get "so busy" that my spiritual enrichment falls by the wayside? Or will I choose to grow by training through the word of God?

{Dear Father, help me to cooperate as you train me to avoid the pitfalls of sin. Thank you for Scripture and the care you have taken to provide instruction for living a blameless life. I pray and give thanks in the name of Jesus. Amen.}

Digging Deeper

- Read **Psalm 119:1**. Underline words and phrases that speak to your heart. Look up the definitions of key words. Write a paraphrase of this verse and make a plan to put God's word into action.
- Do you know the things and situations in your life that put your abstinence in jeopardy? Have you asked God to keep you far, far away from them?
- Use a concordance and find other verses on being blameless. How would you define "being blameless?"

DAY 87

Therefore go and make disciples of all nations, baptizing them in the name of the Father and of the Son and of the Holy Spirit, and teaching them to obey everything I have commanded you. And surely I am with you always, to the very end of the age.
Matthew 28:19,20

PRIMARY PURPOSE

In the rooms of recovery, the primary purpose of the group is to carry the message to the person who still suffers. As an overeater, this would not be possible if I were not abstinent myself. Whenever I tried carrying the message while flip-flopping around in abstinence, it was ineffective. People had heard enough preaching about eating right and losing weight. They needed to see living proof that it could be done. When I got abstinent and stayed abstinent, my effectiveness of "passing it on" soared.

In my Christian walk, the same is true. I have been commanded by Jesus to bring the Good News to all nations. Like in my abstinence, people who are suffering can see through others who are just "talking the talk." My life must be a living testimony of a transformed life. As I yield myself to the Spirit, more and more each day, my effectiveness to bring the gospel to others increases.

What a wonderful thing to have a primary purpose for living! Even when my day seems long and unsuccessful it can be brought back on track by thinking, "I know Jesus. I am called to make Him known." It puts everything in a whole new light. The people around me are no longer seen as "just background noise," they are lambs and potential sheep of my Savior to whom I have been called to treat with love.

{Father, thank you for reminding me that I have a higher calling. Please give me the willingness and the strength to live a life that helps others to be drawn to Jesus. I pray to shine forth love more and more each day. I pray in the name of Jesus. Amen.}

Digging Deeper

- Read **1 John 4:7-21**. Do you know Christians who live out the love of Jesus day in and day out? What might God be teaching you through their life?
- How is your abstinence? Are you "clean, clear, and committed?" Is there one nearby who is suffering from the disease that could be helped by your example? Have you prayed to stay abstinent for your sake and theirs?
- Read these verses about witnessing: **2 Corinthians 5:20; Acts 4:20;** and **Matthew 5:16**. What are they saying to you today?

DAY 88

*So I say, live by the Spirit, and you will not gratify the
desires of the sinful nature.*
Galatians 5:16

LIVING BY THE SPIRIT

Whenever I would binge, the war in my mind and heart
would begin again. It was as if that first compulsive bite
would usher in the great debate: Was I or was I not a compulsive overeater? As I looked for the answer to that question, I
gave myself permission to eat and eat until I knew for sure.
Little did I realize that I was playing right into the hands of
the devil. Eventually I would eat myself into such a state of
depression that I questioned my usefulness to anyone. Deep
despair was very close at hand.

By grace, God came to the rescue. I was given the faith
to embrace the Good News of salvation. Each day now, I am
drawn deeper and deeper into the things of the Spirit. As I
fill up on God's good things, sin is seen to be the rubbish that
it truly is.

There is a saying that "nothing tastes as good as abstinence feels." I now can take that even further: No experience, this side of heaven, can top the life in the spirit! I pray
never to be fooled and used by the evil one again.

*{Dear Father, thank you for opening my eyes to the truth. I
pray to let the Spirit lead me more and more each day. I pray
to stay abstinent for the rest of my life. Strengthen me to keep
in step with the Spirit. I pray in the name of Jesus. Amen.}*

Digging Deeper

- Read **Galatians 5:16**. Make a list of things you could do to "live by the Spirit and not gratify the desires of the sinful nature?"
- Do you still justify your binge eating and not see it as sinful behavior? Read **Romans 6:12-14**. What might God be saying to you through these verses?
- Read about the fruit of the Spirit found in **Galatians 5:22,23**. Look up and define the key words in these verses. Paraphrase these verses and prayerfully plan to apply their teaching.

DAY 89

The body is a unit, though it is made up of many parts;
and though all its parts are many, they form one body.
So it is with Christ. For we were all baptized by one Spirit
into one body—whether Jews or Greeks,
slave or free—and we were all given
the one Spirit to drink.
1 Corinthians 12:12-13

TESTIMONIES OF HOPE

The first few months of abstinence were, at times, quite excruciating. Although I enjoyed seeing my body get smaller as I ate less food, I did not enjoy the emotional pains of life. A few weeks without my "drug of choice" and I saw very clearly why I had become a compulsive overeater. Excess food numbed the pains of life. I overate to check out of the present and go to a place of my choosing.

When life seemed so heavy that I feared losing my abstinence and running back into the food, the "no matter what" stories helped me through and gave me hope. Just knowing that others felt as I felt, yet did not eat, kept me going to the next meal.

As a Christian, life can feel heavy, too. I can get so wrapped up in my circumstances that I forget "whose I am." At these times, my loving Savior does a most wonderful thing—He sends another Christian to share how they came to know Him. As the story of their conversion unfolds, my heart swells with love as I realize that we share the same Spirit and the same hope of glory. Their testimony of hope energizes me to stand firm in my faith. How beautiful is the body of Christ!

{Dear Father, thank you for the care that you show when you keep me from falling. Thank you for my brothers and sisters in Christ who reflect how far reaching and beautiful your love is. I give thanks in the name of Jesus. Amen.}

Digging Deeper

- Read **Acts 22:15.** When did you last share you testimony? What were the circumstances? Would you pray, now, for the willingness and strength to be a bolder witness for Jesus?
- Who are those who encourage you in your abstinence? Have you thanked them lately? Who do you encourage?
- The longest continuous radio drama is a Christian presentation where true conversion stories are re-enacted before a live studio audience. UNSHACKLED can be heard via the web at www.unshackled.org.[7] Why not listen to a testimony today?

DAY 90

This is the day the LORD has made;
let us rejoice and be glad in it.
Psalm 118:24

EMBRACING THIS DAY

The Lord has given you a precious gift: time in this day. You can squander it by obsessing about food, overeating, and/or sleeping off a food hangover. Or, you can remember "whose you are."

You have been redeemed and you belong to Jesus. His Spirit has been placed inside of you. Because of this, when the food calls, you have the power to say, "NO!"

You don't have to live life beaten down and crushed. You have kingdom work to do, and you must refuse to let food abuse stop you in your tracks. You are strong in the Lord, and God wants both your mind and your body to reflect the truth that The King is in control.

{Thank you, Father, for your everlasting goodness and love. Though fears might come and threaten to undo me, I thank You that I can cry out to You and that You will set me free. Please show me where I am still putting my trust in "people, places and things" and not in you. Thank you for giving me Jesus. He is my strength. He has put a new song in my mouth. I pray that my life will always say to the world, "Jesus is my King." It's in His name that I pray. Amen.}

Dig Deeper

- Read **Psalm 118:1-24**. Underline verses and phrases that speak to your heart. Paraphrase one or more of these. Pray to apply today what God's word is saying to you.
- Have you ever written down your salvation story? Bring to mind how the Lord set you free from the power of sin.
- What are your primary fears at this time? Are you willing to lay them down at the foot of the cross?
- Do you have a plan for this day? Will God be glorified in it?
- How is food abuse hindering your work for the Lord today? What are your plans to change this?

Endnotes

1 Written by Darrell R. Brown and Ty Lacy © 2002 Almo Music Corp/ Original Bliss Music (ASCAP) administered by Universal Music Group and Ariose Music (ASCAP) administered by EMI Christian Music Publishing

2 http://www.rbc.org/odb/odb.shtml

3 LIFE APPLICATION STUDY BIBLE, "Submission", (Michigan: Zondervan, 2000), 2203.

4 (as adapted from the Life Application Bible)

5 www.teamministry.com.

6 *The Bible Knowledge Commentary*

7 www.unshackled.org

Breinigsville, PA USA
28 January 2011
254331BV00001B/2/P